THE DAILY TEI
CHRISTI
and to getting

The Daily Telegraph

GUIDE TO CHRISTIAN MARRIAGE

and to getting married in Church

ADRIAN THATCHER

continuum
LONDON • NEW YORK

Continuum
The Tower Building
11 York Road,
London, SE1 7NX

370 Lexington Avenue,
New York, NY,
10017–6503

www.continuumbooks.com

British Library Cataloguing-in-Publication Data
A catalogue record for this book is available from The British Library

ISBN 0–8264–6629–X

Typeset by Fakenham Photosetting Limited, Fakenham, Norfolk
Printed and bound in Great Britain by Biddles Ltd, Guildford and
King's Lynn

For
John and Valerie Thatcher

Contents

Acknowledgments

No book can be written without the help of others. John and Valerie Thatcher, newly married, have been an inspiration. Robin Baird-Smith initiated the project and invited me to write it. Caroline Major has helped me with proof-reading, manuscript preparation and indexing on three books already. This is the fourth to receive her sharp-eyed attention. Sue Burridge advised me invaluably about parts of the final chapter. I gratefully acknowledge their help.

Introduction

You are getting married, or you have a daughter, son, or friend who is about to take this momentous step. You may have decided that you want to have a church wedding, or you may be wondering whether a church service is right for you. Perhaps you are worried about whether you will be welcome in church, or what being married in church really means. Either way, this book is for you for it will tell you everything you need to know about getting married in church.

If you are marrying in 2003 or later you are likely to be at least in your late twenties. In England and Wales in the year 2000, the average age of men marrying for the first time was 30.5 years, and for women 28.2 years.[1] The rising age of marrying couples means that they are likely to bring to their marriages many benefits, including higher or further education, life and work experience, sexual experience, growing maturity, independence from parents, and much reflection on the subject of marriage itself. This book aims to aid that reflection. Just under half of couples where the marriage was the first for both parties chose a religious ceremony.[2] This book is for couples like these, and for couples who are still weighing up the pros and cons of a church wedding.

This is what you will find in the pages of this Guide. Chapter 1 is about marriage as an up-to-date institution. It will show that, despite the myths, married people are happier than single people in all kinds of ways. It compares marriage with other relationships like cohabitation, and shows that marriage is good for husbands, wives, families and society. Chapter 2 tells the story of how marriage has changed and is changing now. Modern societies are much less religious than earlier ones, so we need a simple guide, in language we can understand, to the religious and spiritual side of marriage. This is given in Chapters 2 and 6. Chapter 3 is about what you can do together with your partner to *prepare* both of you for marriage prior to the wedding day. It helps you answer the question, 'Is marriage really right for me?'

Chapter 4 tells the story about what engagement used to mean, and how it once meant that marriage had already begun. It says that marriages and weddings are different. Marriage is a process of deepening and growing commitment in mutual love. A wedding is an event within this process. Chapter 5 will help you plan this event. It goes through actual marriage services used in churches, explains the key points, and discusses what hymns, prayers, readings and music you might want to choose. It deals with awkward questions such as: 'He's an atheist, but I'm an Anglican. What will the vicar say?', or 'I've been divorced, so they won't marry me in church, will they?' Chapter 6 is about maintaining your marriage, once the wedding is over and the photos are on the mantelpiece. Some readers won't bother with Chapter 7, while others will read it first. Why is this? Because it is about marrying again. Suppose you have been through the trauma of a marital breakdown and have got yourself back together again to risk another marriage. What do *you* think about marrying again in church, and what will the church think about you and your request?

Getting married is one of the most exciting and profound things we ever do. Read this book and discover that thinking about and preparing for it is exciting too.

Adrian Thatcher
College of St. Mark and St. John, Plymouth
January 2003

Notes

1. 'Marriage and divorce in 2000, adoptions in 2001', 16 July 2002. Available at www.statistics.gov.uk/releases. Consulted 9 October 2002.
2. 'Marriages, 1991, 1999, 2000: Previous marital status and manner of solemnisation', available at www.statistics.gov.uk/StatBase/. Consulted 9 October 2002.

1

In Praise of Marriage

The advantages of being married

Marriage gets a bad press these days. About 40 per cent of couples who marry now are expected to get divorced.[1] It is possible that your parents' marriage, even if it didn't end in divorce, didn't give you the encouragement to marry that you would have liked. There is always lurid publicity in the media about people's affairs, and the soaps depict cheating, verbal abuse and physical violence as established marital norms. Popular magazines abound with agonies about staying together or splitting up. And many undergraduate textbooks on marriage and family consistently portray a misleading and negative attitude towards marriage, and have been rightly called an 'embarrassment'.[2] Against all this bad publicity, you may be surprised to discover 'an immense body of new research' which shows that, for men and women, 'marriage actually changes people's goals and behaviour in ways that are profoundly and powerfully life-enhancing'.[3] We will be drawing extensively on these in the first part of this chapter. These findings say clearly that marriage is good, or very good, for you. So if you're getting married, you are entering into a social institution ('estate' it used to be called) that is better for you than other 'states' like singleness, cohabitation, serial monogamy, or communes. It is not enough, of course, merely to be married. You have to be married to the right person! But at least you can be assured that marriage as a time-honoured way of living together is likely to be objectively better for you, your children and the common good of society. So in this chapter we are going to look straightaway at these reasons for confidence in marriage. In the next chapter we will enquire more deeply into some of the spiritual and religious meanings of marriage.

Marriage is better than just living together

About 70 per cent of marrying couples in the UK live together first. But about half of all couples who live together split up and don't marry (and this number is getting larger). It is helpful to make a basic distinction between these two types of cohabitors. If you are living with your future spouse, that is called *prenuptial* cohabitation because you are going on to your 'nuptials' or marriage ceremony. If you are not going to get married, then your partner is not a future spouse at all, but your temporary companion or consort. This is *non-nuptial* because you will not be intending to marry and you may be living together as an alternative to marriage.[4] Cohabiting is nearly always a short-term relationship because cohabiting couples usually marry or split. Some couples, of course, will not have decided whether to proceed to their 'nuptials'. If you intend to marry then your relationship probably already resembles marriage, and your commitment to one another will be growing steadily. But what if you have drifted into non-nuptial cohabitation? What can we learn from studies of non-nuptial cohabitation carried out all over the world?

The answer is: your happiness is much more at risk if you are only living together with your partner. The commitment that you are likely to have for one another is much less than the total commitment that belongs to marriage. And that commitment deficit can cause all kinds of problems. Even if you are not fully aware of it your relationship is likely to be 'a "looser bond", with different goals, norms and behaviors'.[5] Cohabiting women are less committed to their partners than wives: and cohabiting men are much less committed to their partners than married men.[6] In a very large sample, cohabitors reported poorer relationship quality than married people, more disagreements, more depression and less satisfaction.[7] Cohabitors are less sexually faithful to one another than spouses, and even when they are faithful they are more suspicious and anxious about their partner's fidelity than are married couples.[8]

Perhaps the most worrying fact about non-nuptial cohabitors is what happens when they get pregnant (as they often do). Cohabitation is a growing source not simply of children, but of *single-parent families*. Recent research in the UK (1997) dramatically proves the connection between them. It indicates that 'about two-fifths of one-parent families headed by never-married mothers are created through childbearing within cohabitation followed by dissolution of the cohabitational union'.[9] In other words: a man and a woman shack up, enjoy sex without commitment, she gets pregnant, he shoves off, she is left holding their baby, and both of them will be left disadvantaged in all kinds of ways. Cohabitation may be attractive to some men just because it is easy to get out of and has few formal responsibilities. And there may be other long-term problems for people who, over time, have lived with several partners ('serial cohabitors'). A study in the USA strongly suggests that the relaxed attitude to cohabitation (less commitment and easy termination) may be carried over into marriage if cohabitors eventually marry. 'Once this low-commitment, high-autonomy pattern of relating is learned, it becomes hard to unlearn.' The marriages, then, as well as the children of non-nuptial cohabitors, are at risk. 'The experience of dissolving one cohabiting relationship generates a willingness to dissolve later relationships. People's tolerance for unhappiness is diminished, and they will scrap a marriage that might otherwise be salvaged.'[10]

Marriage is better for your health . . .

Married people have better physical and mental health than divorced, single, cohabiting or widowed people. If you marry and stay married you are less likely to die from coronary heart disease, stroke, pneumonia, many kinds of cancer, cirrhosis of the liver, car accidents, murder and suicide. Married men live nearly ten years longer than single men. In many societies now, men *of any age group* who are unmarried are about twice as likely to die as husbands! The risk is one and a half times as great for single women, and the health gap between single and married is still growing in developed countries. And the medical evidence for greater marital health is supported by what people report about their perceptions of their own healthiness.[11] In a comparative study of married and unmarried people nearing retirement age, 'wives were about 30 per cent more likely to rate their health excellent or very good than the same-aged single women were and almost 40 per cent less likely to say their health is only fair or poor. Husbands showed similar advantages over unmarried men.'[12]

Married men are better off health-wise than married women, giving rise to the common suggestion that since marriage is better for men than women, marriage is worse for women, and since it is worse for women, women should avoid marriage. This common objection overlooks at least two important factors. The first is that single men engage in a variety of risky activities (like smoking, binge-drinking, drunken and unsafe driving and brawling) that they moderate or abandon when they get married. So their health gain is not at their wives' expense: it is because when they marry they calm down. Secondly, married women live substantially longer lives than single or divorced women, and it is hard to see how they could do this if marriage was bad for them. There is evidence that wives beneficially nag their husbands to abandon risky activities (and husbands beneficially nag their wives to get more sleep and exercise). The emotional support married partners give to each other aids recovery from illness, benefits the immune system, and can affect blood pressure. Because married women have far higher household incomes than unmarried women, they have access to many social goods, like good housing, safer neighbourhoods, a better diet, and so on, and these all contribute to their better health overall.[13]

... and your mental health and happiness

If you marry, your mental health will be better as well. A book by Jessie Bernard in the 1970s[14] argued that women's mental health suffered as a result of marrying, but this book notoriously explained away hard evidence that marriage *benefits* women by saying 'married women only say they are happy because society expects them to say so'.[15] It is one of those books identified above as an embarrassment, and its influence bears no relation to the quality of its argument. While it is not possible completely to separate mental from physical health, it is possible to ask people about their perceived well-being, and social scientists regularly do this. The results are very different from those hypothesized by Bernard. Married people report less depression, anxiety and other types of psychological distress than the unmarried. Widowed and divorced people are three times as likely to commit suicide as married people. According to one survey of 14,000 people over a ten year period, 40 per cent of the married said they were 'very happy with their life in general' compared with the single or cohabiting (less than 25 per cent) or separated (15 per cent).[16] In a study measuring emotional health, 50 per cent of wives described their emotional health as very good or excellent, compared with 38 per cent of unmarried women (the figures were 53: 42 per cent for men). Marriage seems to provide an intimacy and a togetherness that improves mental as well as physical health. Another study reported that 'Married women – regardless of whether they worked or had children – reported greater purpose and meaning in life, and neither work nor children, in the absence of marriage, increased women's feelings of purpose and meaning.'[17] The message could hardly be simpler:

> The emotional support and monitoring of a spouse encourages healthy behavior that in turn affects emotional as well as physical well-being: regular sleep, a healthy diet, moderate drinking. But the key seems to be the marriage bond itself: having a partner who is committed for better or for worse, in sickness and in health, makes people happier and healthier. The knowledge that someone cares for you and that you have someone who depends on you helps give life meaning and provides a buffer against the inevitable troubles of life.[18]

Marriage provides better sex (and more of it)

Recent scientific surveys of attitudes of thousands of men and women towards their sex lives conclude:

> Married people have both more and better sex than singles do. They not only have sex more often, but they enjoy it more, both physically and emotionally, than do their unmarried counterparts. Only cohabitors have more sex than married couples, but they don't necessarily enjoy it as much. Marriage, it turns out, is not only good for you, it is good for your libido too.[19]

Forty-three per cent of the married men, compared with 26 per cent of single men, had had sex at least twice a week. Single men were twenty times as likely to go without sex than married men. Cohabiting couples had rather more sex than married couples, but they did not necessarily enjoy it as much. There are obvious reasons why living together provides more sex. Sexual access to one another is easier than going out and seeking it with a stranger or travelling to a boyfriend's or girlfriend's place and coming back to an empty flat. But married sex is also better sex. Almost twice as many married women as single and divorced women had a sex life that was 'extremely emotionally satisfying'. And husbands and wives are 'significantly more satisfied with sex' than cohabitors.[20]

This difference between married and unmarried in the quality of the enjoyment of sex requires an explanation, and one is ready to hand. It lies in the old-fashioned virtues of love and commitment. 'There are strong reasons for believing that the lifelong, permanent commitment embodied in marriage tends to make sex better.' Married couples take time out to please their partners and satisfy them thoughtfully. 'Love and a concern for one's partner shifts the focus away from the self in a sexual relationship and toward the other person.'[21] The sexual exclusiveness of marriage creates trust. The National Sex Survey in the USA showed that cohabiting men were four times as likely as married men to cheat on their partners. The more partners believed sex outside marriage to be wrong, the more they were satisfied with sex in their marriages. As Waite and Gallagher summarize:

Over the long run, there is no better strategy for achieving great sex than binding oneself to an equally committed mate. For both men and women, marriage as a social institution facilitates the development and maintenance of an emotionally committed, long-term, exclusive union, which typically brings spectacular sexual rewards.[22]

Marriage makes you richer

There are huge financial advantages in being married, and probably more advantages for husbands than wives. Married men are more successful financially than single men at all ages, and the older they are the greater the earnings gap between them. Married men do less housework than their wives. There is a long history of this, but sometimes it remains an agreed policy that, in the marriage, the husband should devote more time to earning for their partners (and their children), while the wife spends more time doing unpaid work at home. This is an example of what is termed 'specialization': the decision to pool resources, allot tasks and assign roles for the greater benefit of the marriage and the family. Married men perform better at the workplace, whereas it makes little difference to the performance of women whether they are married or unmarried. Several studies on housework in the USA indicate that single independent women do 25 hours per week, but married women do a huge 37 hours a week of unpaid work in the home. The reason is simple: children. *Much of the extra work is generated by wives also being mothers.*

The extra housework earning wives do is usually called 'the second shift'. 'When married women cut back on work to care for children, the family may benefit, but the women themselves are taking a risk – gambling that their marriage will last ... Both men and women ... are financially better off because they marry. Men earn more and women have access to more of men's earnings.'[23] (We shall return to the second shift later in this chapter.)

Staying married is much more financially rewarding than splitting up. A study of couples' savings over a five-year period showed that the assets of individuals who had become divorced grew at half the rate of individuals who had remained married.[24] Married people can live much more cheaply than singles and have more capital to invest in their marriage. Married people have in-laws, and they often help out, both financially and in other ways, and especially when children arrive. If there is a divorce the increase in expenditure and decrease in income can be devastating. As Waite and Gallagher summarize:

> When people marry, they are immediately better off, because they now have a claim on not only their own, but their spouses' future income. Over time, the advantages of marriage increase, as couples benefit from higher earnings created by specialization, a lifestyle that encourages savings, the help of a partner in restraining impulse spending, and the reduced costs sharing a life permits.[25]

Marriage is better for the kids

There are many studies which show that children of divorced and single parents do worse than children in intact families. Again, in a summary:

> Children raised in single-parent households are, on average, more likely to be poor, to have health problems and psychological disorders, to commit crimes and exhibit other conduct disorders, have somewhat poor relationships with both family and peers, and as adults eventually get fewer years of education and enjoy less stable marriages and lower occupational statuses than children whose parents got and stayed married.[26]

Robert Whelan's study, based on British data in the 1980s, claimed that children of cohabiting parents were twenty times more likely to be subject to child abuse than children of married parents. If children lived with their mother and their mother's boyfriend who was not their father, they were 33 times more likely to suffer abuse than if they lived with their parents.[27] 'The most unsafe of all family environments for children is that in which the mother is living with someone other than the child's biological father. This is the environment for the majority of children in cohabiting-couple households.'[28] A thought experiment will illustrate what is at stake. Jon Davies envisages an imaginary foetus approaching a life assurance agent about a policy which is most likely to provide him or her with a happy life. The advice given is to get born to a married couple who love each other, and

> avoid, if you can, such 'families' as your biological mother living with a man who is not your father: that tends to be dangerous for you (and for your mother). Money helps, but at every level of society a monogamous, married couple as the family unit will help *a lot* more. It will help you do well at school, to keep out of trouble with the police, and, by example and precept, will teach you the basics of getting on with people, friends and strangers, to learn the necessary sociabilities of proper altruism and sensible egotism, to learn to listen and to talk, to have the courage to get things wrong...[29]

Marriage is safer for women

Domestic violence is an acute and distressing problem, and most of it is perpetrated by men against women and children. Without wishing to detract from its horror and its frequency, it is necessary to point out the hollowness of the domestic violence argument against marriage as an institution which encourages violence. The crucial point is that marriage is much safer for women and children than cohabitation, and many crimes of violence against women in the home are not committed by husbands against their wives, but are perpetrated by partners, lovers, former husbands, former partners, former lovers, and so on. An article by my colleague Lisa Isherwood, entitled 'Marriage: haven or hell' shows just how easy and misleading it is to conflate *marital* violence with *domestic* violence. She combines the category of 'husband' with the category of 'partner' in claiming one in five women is raped by her 'husband/partner' and two women a week are killed in Britain by their 'husband/partner'. She conflates the category of 'wife' with 'partner' in claiming suicide is twelve times higher amongst 'battered wives/partners' (and doesn't mention with whom the comparison is made). Husbands are fortunately omitted from her claim that 'In Scotland 50 women a day, with their children, leave abusive partners', but 'wives' get conflated with 'girlfriends' in the claim that '20 per cent of British men aged 15–25 believe it is acceptable to force sex on women, especially girlfriends/wives'.[30] But these claims, which helpfully draw attention to the problem of domestic violence, unhelpfully perpetuate the myth that marital violence and domestic violence are the same. In fact a government survey in the USA showed that single and divorced women were four to five times more likely to be victims of violence in the home than wives. A sober examination of the evidence shows that throughout the USA: 'Husbands committed about 5 per cent of all rapes against women in 1992–93, compared to 21 per cent that were committed by ex-spouses, boyfriends, or ex-boyfriends, and 56 per cent that were committed by an acquaintance, friend, or other relative.'[31]

Some men, whether husbands or not, practise 'patriarchal terrorism' against women, and their victims are likely to be the ones who seek safety in women's refuges. While marriage as an institution may favour such terrorists, blaming marriage for domestic violence is like blaming motorways instead of drivers for road accidents. Above all children are victims of violence in homes where the biological father is not present. In one careful study very young children were *70 times* more likely to be killed when there was no biological father present in the house but a stepfather or other unrelated man.[32] In the vast majority of cases of domestic violence, it is not marriage, but the forsaking of marriage, that constitutes the problem.

Marriage and the 'common good'

So far, then, we have seen that marriage brings many benefits to couples and their children. But the benefits do not stop there. Society also benefits greatly from marriage, and these benefits are economic and social. Anyone who 'invests' their time, energy and commitment in their marriage can expect to benefit, yet what is undoubtedly true at the 'micro-' level of the family is also true at the 'macro-' level of society. Conversely, if marriage is in trouble, there are many negative social consequences: society suffers. The 'common good' is a term used by theologians and philosophers to invoke a sense of our belonging (the 'common' bit of the 'common good') within a wider community of personal and social relationships (still the 'common' bit). The health of this community (the 'good' bit) depends on how its members contribute to it. The common good is an issue for us at many levels, from what goes on in the local neighbourhood to the creation of new global institutions that one day may be able to prevent wars and require us to live in greater harmony with our polluted and depleted environment. The enemy of the common good is 'the selfish spirit'. This manifests itself in countless ways, e.g., in 'inordinate individualism' or 'self-concern',[33] in the pursuit of economic goals whatever the personal or social cost, in regarding one's neighbour as a rival in the deadly competition for social and educational goods, or in the lack of trust that people display in each other even at the basic familial level. Inordinate individualism means 'that the interests and desires of the individual will take precedence over the interests and desires of one's partner, family, or social group'.[34]

The common good used to be sustained by various institutions. These included churches, social clubs, voluntary action groups, charities, cooperative societies, trade associations, youth groups, uniformed organizations (e.g., Scouts, Guides) and so on. They provided safe places for people to come together for recreation, to engage in social action, to bring about education and the development of character, and often to advance legitimate interests in the face of injustice or oppression. In other words these institutions helped to promote the common good, and the most influential and important of them all was the family. But, as everyone knows, many of these institutions are much weaker than they were, and all have to transform themselves, including marriage and family, if they are to continue to serve the common good. Marriage and family are in great crisis today, but there is no point whatever in bemoaning their demise when energies can be better spent exploiting the new opportunities for marriage and family that the new century provides.

The break-up of tens of thousands of families every year is a national disaster, and the impact of this upon these families, and upon the common good, is almost beyond estimation. In 1996 alone, 162,000 children were involved in divorce.[35] We have already seen the effects of break-ups in terms of declining health and wealth, and the likely and long-term negative impact which divorce has on children. About one birth in every three in Britain takes place outside of marriage, and the life-chances of children brought up by single parents (almost all of them mothers) are significantly and predictably reduced when compared with children of married couples. A report for (and accepted by) the British government in 1999 catalogued some of the social, economic and personal costs of the disintegration of marriage and family:

> Marital breakdown inflicts enormous damage on many of the people involved – not only the couples, but their children, and others – and on society. In 1994 the costs of family breakdown to the public purse were estimated at between £3.7bn and £4.4bn a year. The largest element in that figure was social security spending of between £3bn and £3.7bn. The estimate also included the costs of legal aid, social services, tax allowances and NHS treatment. The cost in legal aid alone was £300m in 1993–4, and this had risen to £468m by 1997/98. It is likely that today public spending caused by family breakdown is running at about £5 billion a year. There are also indirect costs, such as those arising from the damage to children's education, from criminal behaviour and from the impact of breakdown on the use of the housing stock. Nor is it simply a question of financial costs. The human misery resulting from marital conflict and breakdown is immense. For example, divorced men attempt suicide five times more often than married men, and women three times more often.[36]

This report also noted that divorce was seven times as likely to happen in the 1990s than in the 1960s. This escalation of the divorce rate presents an enormous challenge to newly-wedded couples. The second half of the twentieth century saw the liberalization of divorce laws, making it easy to extricate oneself from a difficult marriage. I myself would not wish to see a return to earlier times when the law prevented exit from violent or exhausted marriages. It is essential to be able to get out of marriages where there is, say, abuse, persistent infidelity or untreated drug addiction. The problem, sadly *your* problem if and when your marriage first encounters real difficulties, is whether to avail yourself of the newly acquired freedom of getting out when conflict or difficulty looms. Clearly many couples are 'wanting out' and 'getting out' at the first sign of marital trouble, and the question arises acutely whether this is the best course of action for them.

A very recent study (2002) tracked the paths of 645 spouses who reported living in unhappy marriages in the late 1980s. Some stayed married, others divorced. All of them were re-interviewed five years later. But the expectation that the spouses who had divorced would be happier was unfounded. The study concluded:

> Unhappily married adults who divorced or separated were no happier, on average, than unhappily married adults who stayed married. Even unhappy spouses who had divorced and remarried were no happier, on average, than unhappy spouses who stayed married. This was true even after controlling for race, age, gender, and income.[37]

The study also found that 'Divorce did not reduce symptoms of depression for unhappily married adults, or raise their self-esteem, or increase their sense of mastery', and it concluded that 'Two out of three unhappily married adults who avoided divorce reported being happily married five years later.'[38] Evidence is emerging that divorce is often not a solution but instead the beginning of a raft of new problems.

Another problem that militates against the common good is that marriage is being weakened by the sheer number of couples divorcing, living together informally or having children in single-parent families. There is a danger here of sounding sanctimonious or judgmental, as if married people are morally better than everyone else. To say marriage is being weakened is to observe that merely by living in societies that devalue it one's confidence in it is being subtly undermined in ways which we can be slow to recognize. So: marriage has always involved a commitment until death ('till death us do part'), yet the ready availability of divorce cannot but plant the idea in the minds of marrying couples that they can always get out if the marriage doesn't come up to expectations. So a subtle erosion in our thinking can take place without our even noticing it – marriage is for life, except that it doesn't have to be. What was once understood as an absolute commitment to one's spouse and children, involving deeper responsibilities over time, can become a relative commitment, subject to periodic review and easy termination. Once the degree of commitment is lessened, even the possibility of a long-term relationship is destabilized.

> The meaning of marriage is continuing to evolve. Over time marriage is less often seen as the only acceptable social relationship for sex or coresidence, it is less often considered fundamentally tied to childbearing and chil-drearing, and a gender-based division of labor is less likely to be seen as the only means of economic interdependence among couples. These changes in attitudes, values, and beliefs about many of the social activities closely associated with marriage are closely interrelated with changes in marital behaviors.[39]

Marriage is also weakened by sheer ignorance and misrepresentation. Jessie Bernard's savage attack on marriage is generally disregarded nowadays as bad scholarship, but that doesn't stop people believing her. People live together *instead of* marrying, not because they are morally degenerate but because (at least in part) they do not know that transient relationships of this type may have consequences that do not promote their own, or the common, good. They may even prefer, on moral grounds, to make a limited commitment they can keep, instead of an absolute commitment that they can't. There is almost no sanction against living together outside marriage in Britain. Even the churches have had to get used to it. But the negative side of this remarkable change of social attitude is that people will, and do, think that there is no harm in living together. At one level, of course, there isn't, especially if marriage is intended. But at another level, living in an alternative to marriage undermines marriage, just as having children outside marriage also does. And undermining marriage weakens the common good and contributes instead to the sum of human misery. Once it becomes more socially acceptable say, for biological fathers to distance themselves from the children they sire, fatherhood is itself undermined while motherhood is put under further pressure (as if it wasn't difficult enough for two parents acting together to bring up children).

Closing down the second shift

The single most obvious improvement that must be made to marriage is reducing the 'second shift' for already working wives. This means that the progress made by women in becoming family earners has to be matched by progress made by men in sharing the domestic and caring responsibilities. A recent study of the experience of the first five years of marriage showed that balancing paid work with family responsibilities was the major problem for couples. There was an extraordinary imbalance in the contribution of husbands and wives to doing household tasks. On average, women spend eighteen hours per week, and men one hour on these![40] There can be no going back to fixed and dependent roles for wives. All religions contain assumptions about the dependence of women on men, so we will be returning to this theme in later chapters, drawing attention to how male domination of women might continue to be subverted. But is it still being subverted? If you are soon to be a husband, how do you react to the ideal of the 'new family'? 'New families are being formed, in which men and women share economic responsibilities as well as the domestic tasks that ensure that family members go to work or school clean, clothed, fed and rested, and come home to a place where they provide for each other care and comfort.'[41] According to these authors, the alternative to 'new families' is not a return to 'traditional families' but 'no families' at all, as 'women decide that the new marriage bargain – in which they hold a job and remain responsible for all child-care and housework – is a bad deal, and as men decide that filling all the requirements of a traditional bread-winner but getting few of the traditional prerogatives or wifely supports is just as unattractive'.[42]

A key to successful marriages in the new century will be *negotiation* between the partners regarding every aspect of household maintenance. Two-income families are here to stay, and sharing in the breadwinning will be matched by sharing in the shopping, cooking and cleaning. The parcelling-out to one another of domestic tasks does not have to be equal! Paid work outside the home and unpaid work inside the home together form a 'quantum' or whole. It is this whole that needs to be discussed, reviewed, negotiated and settled. More traditional families settled for 'specialization' which usually created unfair burdens for mothers. Specialization can remain, as long as all the work, inside and outside the home, is fairly distributed. It is essential also that employers cultivate, wherever possible, family-friendly working practices and shifts. It is hard to think of a greater contribution that companies could make to the common good than to reorganize work in order for mothers *and fathers* to be fully involved in child-care arrangements. Flexitime, and proper remuneration, status and promotion for part-time employment all play their part.

Another key to successful marriages is the values and beliefs about marriage which engaged couples bring to their marriage. So bringing to a marriage an open attitude about its duration, or taking advance precautions against failure by signing a prenuptial agreement (see Chapter 3, pp. 53–4) may turn out to be destructive. Marriage vows, as we shall see, are for the rest of your life, and reservations, say, about the totality of the commitment to one's spouse and any children you may have, or about the sexual exclusiveness of the relationship, are likely to influence how the marriage turns out. Beliefs influence behaviour in all kinds of ways. The best insurance against marital breakdown is first not to marry your partner at all unless you want to commit yourself to her or him (and any children you may have) for the rest of your life and second to seek to grow in non-possessive devotion towards your spouse as you learn what 'becoming one flesh' means. More of these themes in later chapters.

Notes

1. In the UK in 1999 there were 145,000 divorces. 'It is predicted that, on current trends, just over two in five marriages will ultimately end in divorce'. The Lord Chancellor's Advisory Group on Marriage and Relationship Support (2002), *Moving Forward Together: A Proposed Strategy for Marriage and Relationship Support for 2002 and beyond*. London: COI Communications, p. 18. Also available at www.lcd.gov.uk.
2. Glenn, N. (1997), *Closed Hearts, Closed Minds: The Textbook Story of Marriage*. New York: Institute for American Values, p. 3.
3. Waite, L. J. and Gallagher, M. (2000), *The Case for Marriage: Why Married People are Happier, Healthier, and Better off Financially*. New York: Doubleday. See also Waite, L. J. (2000) 'Trends in men's and women's well-being in marriage', in Waite, L. J., Bachrach, C., Hindin, M., Thomson, E. and Thornton, A. (eds), *The Ties That Bind*. New York: de Gruyter, pp. 368–92.
4. Thatcher, A. (2002), *Living Together and Christian Ethics*. Cambridge: Cambridge University Press, pp. 45–53.
5. Schoen, R. and Weinick, R. M. (1993), 'Partner choice in marriages and cohabitations', *Journal of Marriage and the Family*, 55 (May): 409. And see Thatcher, *Living Together*, p. 13.
6. Goldscheider, F. K. and Kaufman, G. (1996), 'Fertility and commitment: bringing men back in', *Population and Development Review*, 22 (suppl.): 89.
7. Brown, S. L. and Booth, A. (1996), 'Cohabitation versus marriage: a comparison of relationship quality', *Journal of Marriage and the Family*, 58 (August): 668–78.
8. Waite and Gallagher, *The Case for Marriage*, p. 39.
9. Lewis, J. and Kiernan, K. (1996), 'The boundaries between marriage, nonmarriage, and parenthood: changes in behavior and policy in postwar Britain', *Journal of Family History*, 21 (July): 372–88. And see Lewis, J. (1999), *Marriage, Cohabitation and the Law: Individualism and Obligation*. London: Lord Chancellor's Department Research Secretariat, p. 10.
10. Popenoe, D. and Whitehead, B. D. (1999), *Should We Live Together? What Young Adults Need to Know about Cohabitation*

before Marriage: A Comprehensive Review of Recent Research. The National Marriage Project, Rutgers NJ, State University of New Jersey, p. 5.

11. Waite and Gallagher, *The Case for Marriage*, pp. 47–9.
12. These are Linda Waite's figures published in Juster, T. F. and Suzman, R. (1995), 'An overview of the health and retirement survey', *Journal of Human Resources*, 30 (cited in Waite and Gallagher, *The Case for Marriage*, p. 49).
13. Waite and Gallagher, *The Case for Marriage*, pp. 47–61.
14. Bernard, J. (1972), *The Future of Marriage*. New York: Bantam Books.
15. Glenn, *Closed Hearts*, p. 8.
16. Waite and Gallagher, *The Case for Marriage*, p. 67.
17. Waite and Gallagher, *The Case for Marriage*, p. 76, citing Burton, R. P. D. (1998), 'Global integrative meaning as a mediating factor in the relationship between social roles and psychological distress', *Journal of Health and Social Behavior*, 39: 201–15.
18. Waite and Gallagher, *The Case for Marriage*, p. 77.
19. As summarized by Waite and Gallagher, *The Case for Marriage*, p. 79.
20. Waite and Gallagher, *The Case for Marriage*, pp. 82–3.
21. Waite and Gallagher, *The Case for Marriage*, p. 89.
22. Waite and Gallagher, *The Case for Marriage*, p. 96.
23. Waite and Gallagher, *The Case for Marriage*, pp. 108–9.
24. Waite and Gallagher, *The Case for Marriage*, p. 115.
25. Waite and Gallagher, *The Case for Marriage*, p. 123.
26. Waite and Gallagher, *The Case for Marriage*, p. 125.
27. Whelan, R. (1993), *Broken Homes and Battered Children: A Study of the Relationship between Child Abuse and Family Type.* London: Family Educational Trust.
28. Popenoe and Whitehead, *Should We Live Together?*, p. 8.
29. Davies, J. (1998), 'Neither seen nor heard nor wanted: the child as problematic. Towards an actuarial theology of generation', in M. A. Hayes, W. Porter and D. Tombs (eds), *Religion and Sexuality*. Sheffield: Sheffield Academic Press, p. 332. And see Davies, J. (2002), 'Welcome the Pied Piper', in A. Thatcher (ed.), *Celebrating Christian Marriage*. Edinburgh and New York: T. & T. Clark, pp. 240–9 (242–3).

30. Isherwood, L. (2002), 'Marriage: haven or hell? Twin souls and broken bones', in Thatcher (ed.), *Celebrating Christian Marriage*, pp. 201–17 (201–2).

31. Waite and Gallagher, *The Case for Marriage*, p. 155.

32. Daly, M. and Wilson, M. (1994), 'Some differential attributes of lethal assaults on small children by stepfathers as opposed to genetic fathers', *Ethnology and Sociobiology*, 15: 1–11.

33. On different types of individualism, see Browning, D. S., Miller-McLemore, B. J., Couture, P. D., Lyon, K. B. and Franklin, R. M. (1997), *From Culture Wars to Common Ground: Religion and the American Family Debate*. Louisville, KY: Westminster John Knox Press, pp. 58–9.

34. Thatcher, *Living Together*, p. 30.

35. The Lord Chancellor's Department (1999), *The Funding of Marriage Support – a Review by Sir Graham Hart* (The Hart Report), section 5, available at www.lcd.gov.uk/family/fundingmarsup/reportfr.htm. Consulted 10 October 2002.

36. Lord Chancellor's Department, *The Funding of Marriage Support*, section 9.

37. Waite, L. J., Browning, D. S., Doherty, W. J., Gallagher, M., Luo, Y. and Stanley, S. M. (2002), *Does Divorce Make People Happy? Findings from a Study of Unhappy Marriages*. New York: Institute for American Values, p. 4. Details are available online at www.americanvalues.org. Accessed 18 December 2002.

38. Waite et al., *Does Divorce Make People Happy?*, p. 6.

39. Axinn, W. G. and Thornton, A. (2000), 'The transformation in the meaning of marriage', in Waite et al. (eds), *The Ties that Bind*, pp. 147–65, (160).

40. Center for Marriage and Family, Creighton University, Omaha (2000), *Time, Sex, and Money: The First Five Years of Marriage*. For a description of this, and other excellent publications on marriage (from a Roman Catholic perspective), visit www.creighton.edu/MarriageandFamily/. Accessed 28 October 2002.

41. Goldscheider, F. and Waite, L. J. (1991), *New Families, No Families? The Transformation of the American Home*. Berkeley, CA: University of California Press, p. xiii (cited in Waite and Gallagher, *The Case for Marriage*, p. 171).

42. Waite and Gallagher, *The Case for Marriage*, p. 171.

2

What Does a Church Marriage Mean?

Marriage: the basics

In this chapter we are going to look at the preface to the very recent (2000) Church of England *Common Worship* marriage service. This will get us thinking about some of the basics of a church marriage. Then we are going to have some fun with a saying of Jesus about putting new wine in new bottles (or rather, 'skins'). The idea is that Christian faith is compared with new wine. It's ever fresh, but it needs to mature in new wineskins. I'm going to invite you to think of your marriage as a fine young wine that has to mature in new bottles. We are going to look at some ideas about marriage from the past and the present, and compare them with old and new bottles. Some of these old bottles can be smashed (sorry – recycled), while others will be found admirable for the purpose of maturing your marriage. This parable of Jesus about wine-making explains the rather odd subject-titles in the rest of the chapter.

The *Common Worship* marriage service is a marvellous new service with room for you and your partner to make lots of choices about hymns, readings, prayers, even about some of the wording for your vows. The draft material for the service was used in over 800 parishes before the final version was authorized. The whole service is available on the Church of England website,[1] and an early visit is recommended. Since a majority of marriages in church are held in the Church of England (or

Anglican Church)[2] this is the service you are likely to have at your wedding. If some other service is normally used, you can request *Common Worship* instead. If you marry in a Roman Catholic church or one of the 'free' or 'nonconformist' churches[3] you may be surprised how similar the service is to *Common Worship*. There is also a fine introductory guide to this particular service[4] (which like other formal services in church is also called a 'rite' or 'liturgy'). While churches often disagree with each other about various aspects of Christian teaching, there is substantial agreement among the different churches about what marriage is. So while the *Common Worship* service is Anglican in origin, the teaching it contains is very similar to that in other churches. The preface to the marriage service says:

Marriage is a gift of God in creation
through which husband and wife may know the grace of God.
It is given
that as man and woman grow together in love and trust,
they shall be united with one another in heart, body and mind,
as Christ is united with his bride, the Church.

The gift of marriage brings husband and wife together
in the delight and tenderness of sexual union
and joyful commitment to the end of their lives.
It is given as the foundation of family life
in which children are [born and] nurtured
and in which each member of the family, in good times and in bad,
may find strength, companionship and comfort,
and grow to maturity in love.

Marriage is a way of life made holy by God,
and blessed by the presence of our Lord Jesus Christ
with those celebrating a wedding at Cana in Galilee.
Marriage is a sign of unity and loyalty
which all should uphold and honour.
It enriches society and strengthens community.

No one should enter into it lightly or selfishly
but reverently and responsibly in the sight of almighty
God.

A gift of God in creation

The belief that marriage is a gift of God in creation is written
into the opening prayer of the Methodist marriage service, in
the words:

> Gracious God, your generous love surrounds us,
> and everything we enjoy comes from you.
> We confess our ingratitude for your goodness
> and our selfishness in using your gifts.[5]

In order to understand what the phrase 'gift of God in creation' means, it will be necessary to consult the book of
Genesis in the Christian Bible. Jews and Christians have some
scriptures or sacred writings in common. These are the books
of 'the Old Testament' in the Christian Bible. (I shall refer to
these as 'the Hebrew scriptures', not just because they were
written in Hebrew, but because it is a name for them acceptable
to Jews and Christians.) The first of the Hebrew scriptures is the
Book of Genesis ('the beginning'), and the first two chapters of
this book give us some of the basics of the *Christian* (as well as
Jewish) understanding of marriage.

When Jesus Christ talked about marriage we know he referred
to these chapters in the Hebrew Bible. We find his teaching in
the *Christian* scriptures, or 'New Testament': more precisely it is
found in the first four books or Gospels. When Jesus was in the
middle of a heated argument with some of his religious critics,
he suddenly asked them whether they had ever read 'that in the
beginning the Creator made them male and female?' (Matthew
19:4)[6] He was quoting from the first chapter of Genesis which
says:

> God created human beings in his own image;
> in the image of God he created them;
> male and female he created them.

God blessed them and said to them, 'Be fruitful and increase, fill the earth and subdue it . . . ' (Genesis 1:27–8).

The phrase 'in the beginning' associates marriage with something very old, very fundamental and very basic to human being. Marriage is so ancient that it was created when everything else was! That is why the marriage service says 'Marriage is a gift of God in creation.' Simple! There is no need to read Genesis as if modern science had never happened. We go to the Bible to find a record of how Jews and Christians experienced God. We find there a wonderful collection of literature, some of it in the form of myths and stories. Myths give expression to deeply held insights and truths – they don't have to be rejected because they are not literally true.

Jesus's opponents were referring to the teaching of Moses and the law books of the Hebrew scriptures (the first five books in our bibles). Jesus was pointing out that the teaching about marriage in Genesis 1 and 2 was older than Moses, older than the law, older than the Jewish religion, older even than religion itself. Jesus is saying that when God created the human species, God created marriage along with it! So we can say that even before marriage is a Jewish or Christian institution, it is a basic *human* institution, prior to the countless variations of it in history, tradition, culture, time and place. Sure, the way marriage has been experienced and practised has changed and is changing rapidly at the present time. For instance, the Hebrew scriptures allow polygamy: Christians and contemporary Jews don't. And, of course, marriage isn't needed for everyone to lead a fulfilled human life: Jesus probably wasn't married. The basic point to hang on to is that in Jewish and Christian tradition marriage really is basic to human being, prior to any further elaboration of the meaning of it.

'A unity of heart, body and mind'

Jesus referred to some more verses from Genesis in his teaching about marriage.[7] We will look at these now because they also explain what the marriage service says. The record of his teaching in the Gospel according to Matthew continues:

'Have you never read that in the beginning the Creator made them male and female?' and he added, 'That is why a man leaves his father and mother, and is united to his wife, and the two become one flesh. It follows that they are no longer two individuals: they are one flesh.'

Most of us have a Bible somewhere, so we can check out the passage Jesus talks about for ourselves. Alternatively, you can just log on to <u>www.biblegateway.com</u>[8] (there are lots of other Bible sites) where there are thirteen English translations of the Bible to choose from. In the myth of the Garden of Eden (which starts at Genesis 2:4), the man is made first without the woman, and his loneliness bugs him. God obligingly intervenes to make him a partner: 'Then the Lord God said, "It is not good for the man to be alone; I shall make a partner suited to him"' (Genesis 2:18). There was no creature already made who could do the job properly: 'For the man himself no suitable partner was found' (Genesis 2:20). But God doesn't create the man's partner out of nothing, so to speak, but out of the man's own flesh:

> The Lord God then put the man into a deep sleep and, while he slept, he took one of the man's ribs and closed up the flesh over the place. The rib he had taken out of the man the Lord God built up into a woman, and he brought her to the man. The man said: 'This one at last is bone from my bones, flesh from my flesh! She shall be called woman, for from man was she taken.' (Genesis 2:21–3)

The notion that the married couple is 'one flesh' is very influential in Christian thought. It conveys the idea of sexual union, but there is a lot more to it than just sex. The woman is made from the same stuff as the man, and he recognizes himself in her. (As we would say, they share the same genes.) The personal union which is marriage is made possible because of the structure of the first, mythological, human pair. Marriage is the state of two people belonging to each other as a single unit. When St Paul was thinking about the same passage of Genesis he remarked, 'The wife cannot claim her body as her own; it is her husband's. Equally, the husband cannot claim his body as his own; it is his wife's' (1 Corinthians 7:3–4).

So now we know one of the reasons why the marriage service says 'they shall be united with one another in heart, body and mind': and again, 'Marriage is a sign of unity and loyalty.' The Methodist service declares:

> It is the will of God that, in marriage,
> husband and wife should experience
> a life-long unity of heart, body and mind;
> comfort and companionship;
> enrichment and encouragement;
> tenderness and trust.[9]

The idea that a married couple is a unity, 'one flesh', goes right back through the teaching of Jesus to Genesis. It goes as far back as we can go.

Christ married to the church?

What? I know this sounds plain daft, but hang on a second to see whether we can make any sense of it. Both Genesis and Jesus refer to the practice of the man leaving his father and mother and attaching himself to his wife (Genesis 2:24; Matthew 19:5). (There wasn't much choice for Adam!) Older versions of the Bible use the rich language of leaving and cleaving: 'Therefore shall a man leave his father and his mother, and shall cleave unto his wife: and they shall be one flesh.'[10] (The reference to leaving the home of one's biological parents is significant. It shows how, from earliest times, union with a stranger from outside the home was expected, and the tie or bond between marriage partners was expected to be stronger than the tie or bond of blood between the growing child and his or her parents.)[11] But the Christian scriptures offer a remarkable insight into this further verse in Genesis. In the Letter to the Ephesians (attributed to St Paul), the author discusses marriage in a longer section on relationships between Christians. He too refers back to Genesis 2, just as Jesus had done. This is what he thinks the leaving and cleaving verse means: 'There is hidden here a great truth, which I take to refer to Christ and to the church. But it applies also to each one of you ... ' (Ephesians 5:32).

The author of this letter does not force his insight upon his readers,[12] but his vision of marriage has been influential in the church. He suggests Christians *see the relationship between Jesus Christ and his church as one of marriage*. A favourite term for the church in the Christian scriptures is 'the body of Christ'. Christ is said to have loved the church and given himself up for it (Ephesians 5:25). It is 'his body' (Ephesians 5:30) and husbands are told they 'ought to love their wives, as they love their own bodies. In loving his wife a man loves himself' (Ephesians 5:28). This teaching gives rise to the picture of a divine marriage in which the partners are Christ the bridegroom, and the Church the bride. The outpouring of love which ended up with Jesus prepared to die on the cross for the church and the world, is the standard set for married love (more on this in Chapter 6). Christian marriage is, at its best, a sharing in the relationship between Christ and the church. So: not so daft then, after all? Now we know why the marriage service speaks of Christ being 'united with his bride, the church'. If these ideas stretch your imagination, and you are using the *Common Worship* marriage service for your wedding, why not choose the reading from Ephesians 5 as one of your two or three readings from the Bible? It is one of several that are authorized (just click on 'Readings' when you visit www.cofe.anglican.org/commonworship/marriage/marriage.html and you will find all the authorized readings are printed in full).

New wine, old bottles?

I explained at the beginning of the chapter that there are helpful and less helpful ideas about the marriage in church tradition. While they all have a place in Christian traditions at one time or another, they don't all have a place *now*. The comparison between models of marriage and bottles of newly made wine was triggered by Jesus's tongue-in-cheek observations in the Gospel according to Mark about wine-making. What he said was

No one sews a patch of unshrunk cloth on to an old gar-
ment; if he does, the patch tears away from it, the new

from the old, and leaves a bigger hole. No one puts new wine into old wineskins; if he does, the wine will burst the skins, and then wine and skins are both lost. New wine goes into fresh skins. (Mark 2:22)

In fact this saying may actually be related to marriage, for the preceding verses are about feasting and fasting at a wedding. The suggestion is that Christians have outgrown some (not all!) of the older 'models' of marriage. Following our wine-making metaphor we are about to recycle some old bottles that cannot be expected to preserve the wine that is your marriage!

We are going to compare the preface of *Common Worship* with the preface of an earlier source from the same church: the 1662 Book of Common Prayer. This has been used in Anglican churches ever since 1662, and if you wished, you might persuade the minister who is conducting your wedding to use it (not recommended!). The Prayer Book calls marriage 'holy Matrimony' and says it is an 'honourable estate' and 'commended of Saint Paul to be honourable among all men'.[13] The rite warns against drifting into marriage in rather more graphic terms than *Common Worship*. While the newer text gently advises that 'No one should enter into it lightly or selfishly but reverently and responsibly ... ', the older one says it 'is not by any to be enterprised, nor taken in hand, unadvisedly, lightly, or wantonly, to satisfy men's carnal lusts and appetites, like brute beasts that have no understanding; but reverently, discreetly, advisedly, soberly, and in the fear of God'. The three purposes of marriage are then set out:

First, It was ordained for the procreation of children, to be brought up in the fear and nurture of the Lord, and to the praise of his holy Name. Secondly, It was ordained for a remedy against sin, and to avoid fornication; that such persons as have not the gift of continency might marry, and keep themselves undefiled members of Christ's body. Thirdly, It was ordained for the mutual society, help, and comfort, that the one ought to have of the other, both in prosperity and adversity.[14]

A defence against sin?

We have now entered into a different atmosphere, an older language and, more importantly, a different (although importantly similar) *understanding* of marriage. This 1662 text preserves much of the church's ancient teaching about sex and marriage in the Christian scriptures and throughout most of the church's history. People often assume that the church has always taught what it *now* teaches about marriage. Nothing could be further from the truth! The insistence in the service that marriage is 'honourable' is defensive (and not found in *Common Worship*). It makes sense only against the older assumption that marriage is *dis*honourable, and to be avoided if possible. The better alternative, if one could manage it, is to abstain altogether from sexual experience and therefore to avoid marriage, the institution that legitimizes it. In other words, it is better to be 'celibate'. The seventeenth-century text is wary of sexual desire: the twenty-first-century text speaks enthusiastically of 'the delight and tenderness of sexual union'. While the recent text celebrates sexual love within marriage, the earlier one warns against the perils of lust. There are biblical reasons for this.

In one of his early letters St Paul, who was not married, wrote to the Christians at Corinth, 'To the unmarried and to widows I say this: it is a good thing if like me they stay as they are; but if they do not have self-control, they should marry. It is better to be married than burn with desire' (1 Corinthians 7:8–9).[15] When Paul wrote the letter he believed that Jesus Christ, risen from the dead and ascended into heaven a mere twenty years or so before, would return to earth in his own lifetime. In his view, marriage would be a distraction (1 Corinthians 7:32–8) from the missionary work Christians should be engaging in, in those exceptional times between Christ's first and second comings. Doubtless if Paul had known that Jesus was not coming back within at least the first two millennia of the Church's history, he would have framed a more positive view of marriage. Nonetheless the die was cast. A learned historian of early Christian attitudes to sexuality comments:

> What was notably lacking, in Paul's letter, was the warm faith shown by contemporary pagans and Jews that the

sexual urge, although disorderly, was capable of socialization and of ordered, even warm, expression within marriage. The dangers of *porneia* [casual sex], of potential immorality brought about by sexual frustration, were allowed to hold the center of the stage. By this essentially negative, even alarmist, strategy, Paul left a fatal legacy to future ages.[16]

The negative strategy, characterized by suspicion of sex, concession to human frailty and admission of second-class status is still in place nearly 2000 years later.

Babies make it right?

The first purpose of marriage in the old service is 'the procreation of children'. In the new one, marriage is 'the foundation of family life in which children are [born and] nurtured'. *Common Worship* proclaims the social value of family life. The earlier text is still defensive. Those 'second-class' Christians who married needed a justification for so doing, and having children provided it. St Augustine (354–430), perhaps the most influential theologian of all time, wrote:

> Marriages have this good also, that carnal or youthful incontinence, although it be faulty, is brought unto an honest use in the begetting of children, in order that out of the evil of lust the marriage union may bring to pass some good ... For there is interposed a certain gravity of glowing pleasure, when in that wherein husband and wife cleave to one another, they have in mind that they be father and mother.[17]

Augustine thought that all sexual pleasure was sinful but that God's grace could convert sexual desire into desire for children. Your wedding service will not say this. You will not be discouraged from marriage if you do not want or cannot have children (more about them in the next chapter). In *Common Worship* children are not placed first in the purposes of marriage. The union of the couple comes first and children are born from it and into it. While marriage is said to be the foundation of the family, there is no obligation upon the married to have children.

The second reason for marriage in the earlier text leaves no doubt about the long presence in Christianity of a strand of thought that regards marriage as a concession to the unruly male sexual instinct. Like the reference to the 'brute beasts that have no understanding', the pessimism about the power of sexual desire to mess up sexual relationships or drive us into short-term or inappropriate ones ('fornication' or *porneia*) is paramount. The best way of understanding this strand today is to welcome it as a recognition of the strength of sexual passion, and therefore also for a recognition of the need for the social regulation and personal restraining of the sexual instinct. Marriage provides this, and Christians looking for biblical evidence for the social usefulness of marriage in controlling desire found it (once more) in St Paul's teaching. Some of the Christians at Corinth had expressed an even more extreme view about sexual experience. They taught 'It is a good thing for a man not to have intercourse with a woman.' (1 Corinthians 7:1). Paul's answer was 'Rather, in the face of so much immorality, let each man have his own wife and each woman her own husband' (1 Corinthians 7:2). Marriage is a 'concession' (1 Corinthians 7:6), a half-way position between outright celibacy and the social norm that it undoubtedly is today. Husbands and wives should try to avoid sexual intercourse, but not to the extent that their frustration would lead them to seek relief elsewhere! 'The husband must give the wife what is due to her, and equally the wife must give the husband his due' (1 Corinthians 7:3).

'Marital debt'?

From Augustine on, this was called 'the marital debt'[18] that had to be paid on demand. But the economic metaphor is, to say the least, unfortunate. It makes even the desiring of one's spouse fraught with tension and regret, and the temporary satisfaction of this desire an unfortunate and unpleasant necessity. Don't you think there is a huge contrast between the grim pessimism of the older text and the reference to 'the delight and tenderness of sexual union' in the newer one? The phrase 'such persons as have not the gift of continency' (self-restraint) in the older text continues the concessionary theme. In *Common Worship* it is marriage not celibacy that is the gift ('a gift of God in creation', 'The gift of marriage brings husband and wife together'). Times really have changed! And for the better!

There are some old bottles here, then, that won't hold the new wine of marriage. But the third reason for marriage, 'the mutual society, help, and comfort, that the one ought to have of the other, both in prosperity and adversity' doesn't need to be recycled, does it? It looks like a recipe for a mutual partnership of equals in friendship and is sometimes called the 'friendship model' of marriage.[19]

Old wine, new bottles?

I was warned at school never to mix my metaphors, but I'm going to risk doing so now. If marriage is like new wine, it needs to be stored in new bottles so it can mature. But what if marriage is like *old* wine that has matured already? It will already *be* in bottles that have grown old with it. In this section we are going to taste some fine old wines. I mean there are powerful ideas about marriage that really are of excellent vintage. They are not just enjoyable to taste – they are essential for you to appreciate the full, rich flavour of a lasting marriage.

Consent

The Christian church was content to take over from the Jewish and pagan worlds, the legal framework for marriage, and even the ceremonial rites, appropriately Christianized.[20] There was no requirement to marry in church. Girls could marry as early as twelve and be betrothed as young as seven! Marriages in the first millennium (and continuing into the second) were likely to have been *arranged* between the families of the bride and groom. (We in the West would do well to remember that our practice was once similar to cultures that practise arranged marriages now.) The arrangement of marriages by families leads to a very important change in the history of Western marriage. The coercion of some young women and men into marriages they did not desire led over time to the view that marriage should be con-tracted by the exchange of consent between the two spouses alone. This change begins around the ninth century, but took longer to become recognized in the laws of the Church.[21] The vow made by the bridegroom in the *Common Worship* service starts with the words 'I, *John* , take you, *Jane*, to be my wife ... ' This is known as the exchange of consent, and it must be said in the present tense because it is a 'performative' statement (that is, you do something by saying something), and if it was said in the future tense ('I will take' ...) it would be a promise of a taking in the future, and not a vow. The substance and language of this vow has remained constant over three millennia (more on this in Chapter 5).

A sacrament

Another important change to marriage in the second millen-nium is that it becomes a *sacrament*. Around the twelfth century, the church taught that it was one of seven sacraments.[22] An official definition of sacraments (in the *Catechism*[23] of the Catholic Church) is that they 'are perceptible signs (words and actions) accessible to our human nature. By the action of Christ and the power of the Holy Spirit they make present efficaciously the grace that they signify.'[24] Christians believe that when, say, you receive holy communion or baptism, something happens at a much deeper level than the surface appearance of what is going on. On the same reasoning they think that when you marry in church, something again happens at a much deeper level than the surface appearance of what is going on. 'Grace' means that God's power and love comes to you in a special way (even though you may be unaware of it until later). In the great upheavals of sixteenth-century Europe called 'the Reformation', the 'Protestant' churches and the Church of England broke away from the Roman Catholic Church, and one of the things they disagreed about was whether marriage was a sacrament. The 1662 Prayer Book called it 'holy Matrimony', 'an honourable estate', and said God 'ordained' it. *Common Worship*, as we have seen, calls it 'a gift of God', 'a way of life made holy by God' and 'a sign of unity and loyalty'. But a sacrament it isn't!

There are two points about this controversy that I want to emphasize. Almost unbelievably, the reason why marriage was declared a sacrament was because it was thought that God's special grace was needed to control desire and convert it into the desire for children. A great Roman Catholic historian spills the beans on this:

> Everyone knew what goes on in marriage: erotic love, bodily passion running out of control, sin-infected flesh satisfying itself sexually. There is grace given in the sacrament, so the explanation went, but it is not sanctifying [doesn't make you holy]; it is medicinal. It is a divine help for keeping passion not only inside one's marriage, but even within it confined to the innocent and therefore permissible motive for having intercourse, which is to conceive a child.[25]

Sacramental grace is the medicine for the sickness of lust. No sensitive Christian would speak like this today. This really is mouldy old wine! The grace God gives in marriage is more likely to be explained today in terms of the hallowing (or making holy) of the human love of the couple so that the overflowing Love which God is, touches it, makes it deeper and long-lasting, and brings it to expression in many practical ways. Now we know why the *Common Worship* preface says it is a gift 'through which husband and wife *may know the grace of God*'. The second point about the controversy is that in the present century many Christians frankly can't be bothered whether marriage is called a sacrament or not, and that is because they are united about something more important. They believe that when you marry, God *blesses* your marriage. You do and you will receive God's grace. Experts will disagree about whether God's grace is 'channelled' through the exchange of consent, the blessing the priest gives when he or she pronounces you married, or the 'consummation' of your marriage in love-making. I think God's grace comes both 'in the delight and tenderness of sexual union' and in the 'joyful commitment to the end' of your lives. Everything you do in the ceremony can be a sign of your wider, life-long partnership, and that is where God's grace will be found. (More on this in Chapter 6.)

A covenant

A deservedly popular model of marriage in contemporary Christian thought is based on the idea of a covenant. The term is implied (but not stated) throughout the preface we have been examining, especially in the phrase 'joyful commitment to the end of their lives'. There is a small block of text in *Common Worship* that is intended to be read by the waiting congregation before the service starts, which says marriage is 'based upon a solemn, public and life-long covenant between a man and a woman'.[26] (You could put this in your Order of Service if you wanted.) The Roman Catholic Church teaches that marriage is a covenant, 'the matrimonial covenant, by which a man and a woman establish between themselves a partnership of the whole of life', and Protestants go along with that completely.[27] This is a very big idea. Christians believe God has formed a covenant with us (i.e., humanity), and our home (i.e., the earth). An older word for covenant is 'testament', and the old and new testaments in the Bible express the belief that God formed two covenants, one with the Jewish people, and a new one with everyone and everything. It is the new covenant to which Christians witness. It means God's infinite care for everything is constant, no matter what, no matter how much people clag it up, and no matter whether people believe in God or not.

The big idea is that marriage too is a covenant. And there's more. When husbands and wives start loving each other a little like God loves everything and everyone, they touch base with God's love. They learn a bit about what God's divine love is when they celebrate their own human love for each other. That is another reason why faithfulness is emphasized in Christian marriage. Human faithfulness mirrors God's own faithfulness. The *Catechism* puts it well when it speaks of 'the Good News that God loves us with a definitive and irrevocable love, that married couples share in this love, that it supports and sustains them, and that by their own faithfulness they can be witnesses to God's faithful love'.[28] Covenants are not supposed to be broken. You will make your covenant with your partner when you exchange consent and make your vows. All covenants have witnesses. (You will need the signatures of three witnesses at your wedding to make it legal.) God will be the first witness of your marriage covenant, and God's signature on your marriage is the grace bestowed on you in your life together. 'Covenant' makes sense of that steadfast commitment which is love. A couple marrying in the Middle Ages could expect to come to love one another: they would not expect to love one another *before* they exchanged consent (especially if their partner had been chosen for them). There is no mention of human love in the Preface to the marriage service in the Book of Common Prayer; whereas in the *Common Worship* preface it occurs three times.

A commonwealth

We've already noted how the future of marriage is bound up with the common good, but did you know that in the seventeenth century marriage was also called a common *weale* or common *wealth*? This was really another and an earlier way of saying that marriage provided personal *and social* benefits, that it contributed to the 'common good' of society. An Anglican pamphlet of 1598 called *A Godly Form of Householde Gouernment* began with the words 'A household is as it were a little *commonwealth*, by the good government whereof, Gods glorie may bee aduanced, the common-wealthe whiche standeth of several families, benefited, and all that live in that familie, may receiue much comfort and commoditie.'[29] Now we know why the Preface loudly proclaims marriage 'enriches society and strengthens community'. It is an old insight with new relevance for postmodern times – definitely old wine in an old bottle.

A party

There is a remarkable story to check out in the Gospel according to John (John 2:1–11). Jesus is at a wedding reception where there are big drinkers. When the wine runs out Jesus made more wine from some water – lots more wine, in fact over 800 litres, or 1,000 bottles of it (John 2:6). This will also make a great reading at your ceremony (and one which has been used at Christian weddings over the centuries). The Preface to *Common Worship*, you recall, said that marriage was 'blessed by the presence of our Lord Jesus Christ with those celebrating a wedding at Cana in

Galilee'. St John said it was Jesus's first miracle, and part of the significance of the miracle is that Jesus shares in the joyful celebration, and blesses and enhances it. We shouldn't be surprised about this. Jesus uses the picture of a royal wedding reception to explain what the kingdom of Heaven is (Matthew 22:1–14).[30] The great victory over evil at the end of time is symbolized as a 'wedding banquet' (Revelation 19:9). I have been to wedding receptions where I have thought that the general merriment carried just as much spiritual meaning as the marriage service itself, just because Christians really do celebrate marriage 'as a gift of God in creation' and want to express this appropriately when their loved ones and friends marry. This sort of celebration deserves to be wholehearted.

I hope the idea of making, storing and drinking wine in this chapter has appealed to you (sorry if it has confused you!). The story of Jesus at the wedding reception was deliberately written by its author to encourage us to find our own meanings in it.[31] It is another passage in the Christian scriptures where wine is associated with weddings (and not just with the mass, or holy communion). This story, and the saying about new bottles for new wine, enabled us first to compare your marriage with a bottle or bottles of wine, that need to be cared for by being stored in new bottles. We pressed this comparison when we noticed some old bottles in which we would not want to store our marriage. Next we compared some Christian ideas about marriage with *old*, vintage wine, and suggested these needed to be tasted for ourselves in order to have a successful marriage. Finally the partying at a wedding reception Jesus went to, which probably went on for several days, encourages us to think of our own marriage as a source of celebration and joy, a sacrament by which we learn something of the love of God through our love for each other. Whether the momentous step of becoming married is *for you*, or not, is the subject of the next chapter.

Notes

1. www.cofe.anglican.org/commonworship/marriage/marriage.html.
2. In Wales, the Anglican Church is the Church of Wales; in

Scotland, it is the Scottish Episcopal Church; in Ireland, it is the Church of Ireland.

3. Among the best known are the Methodist, Baptist, United Reformed and Presbyterian churches.

4. Lake, S. (2000), *Using Common Worship: Marriage – A Practical Guide to the New Services*. London: Church House Publishing.

5. *Methodist Worship Book*. Peterborough: Methodist Publishing House (1999), p. 368.

6. Unless otherwise stated, the version of the English Bible used is *The Revised English Bible*. Oxford and Cambridge: Oxford University Press, Cambridge University Press (1989).

7. Matthew 19:5–6, quoting from Genesis 2:24.

8. Accessed 16 October 2002.

9. *Methodist Worship Book*, p. 369.

10. Genesis 2:24 in the Authorized Version of the Bible (1611).

11. See Peachey, P. (2001), *Leaving and Clinging: The Human Significance of the Conjugal Union*. Lanham, MD: University Press of America.

12. As far as we know and expect, all biblical authors were men.

13. The biblical reference is to Hebrews 13:4. (It is now accepted that the letter to the Hebrews was not written by St Paul.)

14. There are several online versions of the 1662 Book of Common Prayer. The one I have used here is www.eskimo.com/~lhowell/bcp1662/. Accessed 14 October 2002.

15. St Luke's attitude to marriage may have been even more negative. In a saying he attributes to Jesus, he hints that people who marry in this world forfeit their place in the next! See Luke 20:35.

16. Brown, P. (1989), *The Body and Society: Men, Women and Sexual Renunciation in Early Christianity*. London: Faber & Faber, p. 55.

17. Augustine, *On the Good of Marriage*, Chapter 3. The translation used here is from P. Schoff (ed.) (1887), *The Nicene and Post-Nicene Fathers*, Buffalo, IL: Christian Literature Co., pp. 399–413 (p. 400).

18. *On the Good of Marriage*, Chapter 4.

19. See Thatcher, A. (1999), *Marriage after Modernity: Christian*

Marriage in Postmodern Times. Sheffield: Sheffield Academic Press, pp. 217–22.

20. For a discussion of some of the main changes to betrothal and marriage in Christian history, see Thatcher, A. (2002), *Living Together and Christian Ethics*. Cambridge: Cambridge University Press, Chapters 5 and 6.

21. Brooke, C. (1989), *The Medieval Idea of Marriage*. Oxford: Clarendon Press, pp. 129–38.

22. On Protestant and Catholic attitudes to marriage as a sacrament, see Thatcher, *Marriage after Modernity*, pp. 232–48.

23. A book that elaborates the teaching of a church.

24. *Catechism of the Catholic Church*. London: Geoffrey Chapman, (1994), para. 1084, p. 249. The *Catechism* is an official handbook produced by the Roman Catholic Church describing its teaching for all interested people, whether Roman Catholics or not.

25. Mackin, T., SJ (1982), *What is Marriage?* New York: Paulist Press, p. 32.

26. Lake, *Marriage*, p. 33. If you marry in an Anglican church, the priest is likely to keep copies of this.

27. In Protestantism the idea is expounded by the sixteenth-century reformer, John Calvin. See Witte, J., Jr (1997), *From Sacrament to Contract: Marriage, Religion, and Law in the Western Tradition*. Louisville, KY: Westminster John Knox Press, pp. 74–129.

28. *Catechism of the Catholic Church*, p. 369, para. 1648.

29. Witte, *From Sacrament to Contract*, p. 167.

30. Read this to find out what happened to the guests who refused the invitation!

31. If you would like to read a profound meditation on this story, and find out more about the meaning of marriage in the Orthodox Church, try Fotiou, S. (2002), 'Water into wine, and *eros* into *agape*: marriage in the Orthodox Church', in Thatcher (ed.), *Celebrating Christian Marriage*, pp. 89–104.

3

Preparing for Our Marriage

How do we prepare for our marriage?

Becoming married is the most important step we may ever take,
yet we are mostly underprepared for it. Perhaps with better
preparation marriages would be more honest, richer and longer
lasting. In this chapter we are going to ask how we can prepare
for marriage. Some searching questions are raised which you and
your partner might want to think about for yourselves, both separately and together. They can be conveniently arranged under
the heading of the five 'C's – communication, commitment,
conflict-resolution, children and career. For some there is a sixth
'C' – church. We will also examine some 'premarital inventories'
– sets of questions that can be purchased and used either with
your partner or a specially trained person. The use of premarital
inventories is increasingly popular. Would it be helpful for you
both to undertake one of these? But first, two prior questions:
what preparation can you expect from the church for your
church marriage? And, before we think about preparing for
marriage, is marriage right for you – or not?

Churches vary in the quality and quantity of the marriage
preparation they offer. If one of you is a Roman Catholic and
you marry in a Roman Catholic church, you will normally be
required to attend a series of meetings or classes. You will be
likely to meet other couples. There will be videos and publications, and perhaps a weekend away. In the Roman Catholic

Church, marriage is a sacrament, and divorce is unavailable. These are two reasons why that church invests heavily in marriage preparation. In the Church of England and the free churches marriage preparation for couples is more haphazard. It is organized at parish or local church level. You can expect, before the wedding but after your initial approach to the minister, two or three meetings with him or her (it is nearly always the minister who prepares you who will marry you). But since one of these will be about the legal and paperwork details, and one will be a rehearsal, there won't be a lot of time for the minister to explain the meaning of the service. That is why you are advised to do some of this for yourselves. (Reading this book is a good start!) A recent research project on the provision of marriage preparation among 400 churches in the south of England revealed there was a one in three chance of some couples receiving no preparation at all, while the average number of sessions couples were involved in preparation was 3.6.[1] It is probably right to suggest that most marriage preparation is *wedding* preparation, and that is something quite different.

The 'vocation' to marriage

We have seen that marriage is a gift of God in creation, but is it a gift that everyone should gratefully receive? The Christian answer to this question has been a consistent 'No'. Monks, nuns and celibate priests (in the Roman Catholic Church) all witness to the value of the single life. The bishops of the Church of England say, 'The first thing the Christian will want to say to the single is that Jesus himself was single. Any idea that to be unmarried is to fall short as a human being is totally false. On the contrary, the heart of what it is to be human was shown to us in one who never married.' They then go on to describe some of the reasons why some people make singleness a positive choice. These include the desire for privacy or independence, a condition of their work, care for dependants, or (quite simply) that they were open to marrying but never met the right person.[2] It is not necessary to marry to live a fulfilled, useful and happy life! So, should I – perhaps even *could* I – marry?

One way of getting inside this question is to think, with Christians generally, of marriage as a *vocation*. A vocation is a 'calling'. People who become priests and ministers believe that God has 'called' them to these sacred tasks, or, as some Christians say, 'holy orders'. Protestant Christians extended the idea of a calling to secular professions. God might be calling you to be a doctor, or a teacher, or an engineer, or a gardener. The experience of being called to a profession or task today is unlikely to be a literal hearing of a voice taken to be the voice of God, or a vision where one believes it is God or God's messenger one sees. It is more likely to be a combination of factors which include an honest recognition of one's abilities, desires (and weaknesses!) and an honest seeking to perform the will of God, or follow Christ or his example of love for and service to humankind. It is these beliefs that result in large numbers of Christians entering the caring professions or undertaking voluntary work in civil society,[3] and it is usual for large decisions like these to be accompanied by private prayer. In calling marriage a vocation, similar questions about skills, desires and obedience to God are asked. For instance, have I what it takes to be a good, faithful wife or husband? Could I keep the vows I will have to make? Why not consider alternatives to marriage? There is a way of answering the question 'Am I called to marriage?' for yourself. That is to assess how, if or when you marry your fiancé(e) you shape up to the five 'C's.

The five 'C's

Since about 40 per cent of marriages break down, researchers now know a great deal about what goes wrong. Some of the causes of 'marital distress' and possible breakdown include difficulties in communicating with one another, prior cohabitation (on this see Chapter 4), previous experience of divorce (of self, partner or parents), marrying young, rushing into marriage, disharmony with in-laws or friends, having different beliefs and values, disagreement over careers (generally hers), whether to have children, intolerance of the 'second shift', and so on. It seems to follow that if signs of future 'marital distress' can be detected in advance, it may be possible to do something about them now. On the other hand, they may provide a painful but valuable piece of self-knowledge leading to the conclusion that you may not be 'called' to marriage after all.

You could begin gently by logging on to a conservative, but valuable Christian website that is all about getting married, www.marriageresource.org.uk and selecting 'Choosing a Marriage Partner'. There you will find 'points to consider' if you currently have a prospective marriage partner (the website coyly calls them 'friends'). It is important to stress that many of these points are downright naïve, and they are meant to be. That is because even the simplest questions about partners tend to be evaded or even suppressed. Here is a sample:

- Ask yourself is my friend attentive to my needs? Also, ask yourself am I as concerned for my friend as I am for myself?
- Are you comfortable with each other – can you really relax in each other's company? Can you be your real self in front of your friend or are you always trying to be someone else (more exciting, witty, etc.)?
- Can you accept that nobody is perfect? Are your standards for your friend too high for them to live up to? Try not to be too idealistic.
- Does your friend forgive you easily if you upset them and can you forgive them when they upset you? Feelings of resentment and anger are dangerous when harboured. Resolve conflict as soon as it rears its ugly head.
- How well do you get on with your potential in-laws? Discuss the future of family ties outside of marriage, before you get too involved.
- Can you trust your friend's financial handling/track record? Do you feel you ought to keep a separate account because you don't trust their spending habits? Try to discuss financial problems in the open and decide on a plan of action to remedy the situation.
- If you plan to have children, watch how your friend interacts with other people's kids. Will he/she make a good father/mother? Are they kind, caring and gentle?
- How important is it to you to share routine tasks such as doing the washing up, putting the bin out, washing the car

and going food shopping. Be realistic about who can do what, depending on who works longer hours. If, however, it is important to you to share the mundane tasks be honest about it and decide who does what.[4]

These are uncomfortably obvious questions, but they should all be asked before solemn vows are made. A recent research report on distressed couples in the first five years of marriage showed clearly that the chief problems besetting young marriages are balancing jobs and career with family life, frequency of sexual relations and debt.[5] So: *time*, *sex* and *money* (the title of the report) are the biggest problems. 'Pre-emptive' attention to these prospective problems may stop or at least mitigate them in married life. And, of course, without good *communication*, there can be no in-depth discussion about anything.

Communication

Marriage is above all a *dynamic* relationship. That means that as spouses grow and mature, their marriage also grows and matures. Conflict, if it is articulated and effectively dealt with, can actually be an aid to mutual understanding and a constructive spur in the growth of a mature, fulfilling marriage. But, as we all know, conflict is hard to deal with, and when it is allowed to fester, the marriage itself can become poisoned. Perhaps we all need to learn some skills which help us to interact better with our partners? Since in marriage we intend to stay with our partner for life, learning to communicate effectively may be the best marital investment we ever make. There are many books (and courses) on this subject, and there is space here only to suggest how we can learn to communicate better with one another. One of the single-day workshops, widely attended in the USA (C-PREP) teaches couples about four 'danger signs' which may disrupt communication, and how to deal with them.[6] The first is *escalation*, and it happens when you get angry with each other, perhaps raising your voice, or making accusations. The skills needed here are to control the discussion, or, if that fails, to leave it, not by walking away but by suggesting a cooling-off period and saying sorry for any hurt that has already been caused. A second danger sign is *invalidation*, 'a pattern in which one partner subtly or directly puts down the thoughts, feelings, or character of the other'.[7] There are countless ways through which couples can undermine or destabilize each other, often by casual but wounding remarks. Invalidation must be unlearned, and *validation*, the positive affirming of one's partner practised instead.

A third danger sign is *negative interpretation*, and this happens whenever one partner construes what the other may have said or done in a poor light, or refuses to give him or her the benefit of the doubt. A fourth danger sign is *withdrawal* or *avoidance*. John Gray, in his famous book *Men are from Mars, Women are from Venus*, argues convincingly that men and women react differently to conflict. Martians walk away and 'go to their caves to solve problems alone', while 'to feel better Venusians get together and openly talk about their problems'.[8] So Venusians feel ignored, and when Martians get summoned from their caves, they feel their need for privacy is being violated. Both sexes practise withdrawal at times, but men practise it notoriously. Merely being more aware of how we are likely to react when discord arises, and how our reaction may be understood by our partner, is a first and generally effective defence against its escalation. Negative interactions can, and often do, accumulate, and inflict serious damage on the relationship. If you notice these danger signs in your relationship already, perhaps you should see them as real dangers to the prospective marriage. Some of these may be character traits which you or your partner may have acquired as a result of experiences when you have been at the sharp end of others' anger, or been invalidated, or put down. Perhaps if you notice these danger signs in yourself over a considerable period of time, marriage is not your vocation.

Communication skills do not operate at the level of language alone. We are all probably familiar with the term 'non-verbal communication', and the most obvious example of non-verbal communication (although it will also involve words!) is love-making. The couples in the *Time, Sex and Money* report made love only six or seven times a month for the first two years of marriage, and this figure dropped to three or four times a month after five years. Are you surprised? The 'delight and tenderness' of the marriage service Preface presupposes that touching and caressing, arousing and playing, climaxing and subsiding are all saying something, and if there is distress in the relationship then love-making can take on the tensions in the marriage and make them worse, or, alternatively, it can help to heal them. Making love is a language, and sometimes what we 'say' when we do it can be anything but loving. Indeed the famous psychiatrist and Roman Catholic Jack Dominian (in a highly recommended and very readable book) rightly calls love-making a *divine* language.[9] He describes sexual intercourse as

> a language, in which the couples are speaking to and com-municating with each other with their bodies. This is a communication of love. It is a language that shifts the individual from egoism to a mutuality of sharing. They are sharing each other. It is a language that shifts the tech-nology of pleasure to mutual commitment. And finally, it is a shift from potentially meaningless pleasure to mean-ingful interaction. Thus the physical becomes a channel of communication for the personal. This personal communi-cation develops over time. As the couple move from being in love to loving, and as the loving changes with time, so sexual intercourse speaks a different language.[10]

I think this is right. All Christians believe that God is love (and the Christian scriptures say so directly).[11] If you marry in an Anglican church, you may be given a 'teaching document' called simply *marriage* (oddly the title has no capital). The document starts by saying:

> God is love (*1 John 4.16*), and in creating human beings he has called us to love, both himself and one another. The love of God the Father for his Son is the ground of all human love, and through the Holy Spirit we may dwell in that love, which the Son has shown to us (*John 15.9*).[12]

One of the surer ways of learning of the love of God is through the delight and tenderness of human love. That love is often at its most intense as couples prepare to make a life-long commitment to one another. Making love is more than pleasure. It is communication. As Dominian says, every time a couple make love, 'they are saying to each other, "I recognise you. I want you. I need you. I appreciate you."[13]

Commitment

This is the second 'C'. We have seen how Christian marriage is a mutual commitment between a man and a woman which 'models' the commitment of Jesus Christ to the church. While human commitments can only begin to resemble the commitments which God has for the world and Christ has for the church, the best human commitments are permanent, faithful and exclusive. So choosing a partner is quite unlike choosing a commodity that is replaceable, or renewable after fair wear and tear. Your spouse is your partner for life and both of you when you enter Christian marriage should be aware that the commitment you make is unconditional. A commitment that is less than unconditional is not marriage. So a provisional or a conditional commitment is something else. A limited commitment which resorts to termination when trouble looms is not what Christians mean by marriage.

The insistence on total, faithful, life-long commitment to our spouse is thought to mirror the commitment of God to humankind. It provides a stable context for children and a space for spouses to be themselves and to develop mutual trust. So this is another test about the vocation to marriage. Are you ready for this kind of commitment with your intended spouse? In the last decade it has become customary to distinguish between two types of commitment – commitment as *dedication* and commitment as *constraint*.[14] The first kind of commitment is devotion to the partner for the partner's sake, not just for oneself. It is long-term and for that reason it seeks to deal with short-term difficulties for the sake of the long-term relationship. The second kind of commitment is motivated by external factors. So, in a temporary but painful crisis, one might contemplate becoming divorced, but the commitment of constraint prevents one from doing so, and for reasons other than dedication to one's partner. It might, for example, be fear of what one's peers might think, or worry about the costs of divorce, or about the effect on the children, that keeps the marriage together. The important point about constraint commitment is not to under-rate it. It can actually have a beneficial effect during times when the marriage is in a temporary crisis. It can help both parties hang on and work for better things. Our problem is that in societies where divorce is common and readily accepted constraint commitment is weak. While it can never be the basis of a good marriage, it can – if it is ever allowed to be – an aid to the preservation of a good marriage.

The emphasis on permanent life-long commitment in the Christian faith cannot always be completely reconciled with the growing practice in the USA of taking out prenuptial agreements before the wedding ceremony. A prenuptial (or 'pre-marital' or 'antenuptial') agreement (a 'prenup' for short) is a legal contract taken out by prospective spouses that establishes what happens to their income, assets, and debts if the marriage ends in divorce, separation or death. Prenuptial agreements are not yet recognized in British law, but the problems which give rise to prenuptial agreements as attempted solutions confront most marrying couples, and the reasons for avoiding them, in many cases, helpfully illustrate the kind of commitment that marriage requires. Many couples in the USA, especially if a second or subsequent marriage for one or other of them is involved, take out a prenuptial agreement in order to establish the rights and responsibilities of each partner. The agreement can set out the rules for virtually every aspect of a marriage, including deciding who is responsible for household bills and expenses. An obvious advantage, in the case of second or subsequent marriages, is that the inheritance rights of children from a previous marriage can be stipulated in advance, and each spouse may, if desired, waive the right to inherit from the other's estate.

One reliable Internet source suggests you should consider a prenuptial agreement if either or both of you:

- have children or grandchildren from a previous marriage
- own a business or are a partner in a business, law firm, or medical practice

- possess significant assets or property
- have much more money than your prospective spouse – over twice as much is the rule of thumb
- plan to support the other through college or a professional school
- have significant debt.[15]

But the main problem with prenuptial agreements is that they may be the outcome of an attitude to marriage that can be destructive by eroding the determination to keep the marriage vows. They can function as a misguided insurance policy against divorce. There should surely be no moral objection to the desire to make provision, say, for children of a previous marriage, or to limit the liability of a second spouse for debts and responsibilities incurred before the wedding. This is similar to making a new will. So, it would be foolish to issue a marital health warning against all prenuptial agreements. It is possible to argue that just as taking out house contents' insurance doesn't make it more likely you will be burgled, so taking out divorce insurance doesn't make it more likely your marriage will collapse. But this is a misleading comparison. Christian marriage is an unconditional commitment 'till death us do part', and a prenuptial agreement requires a marrying couple to contemplate ending their marriage before it has even begun. While a will specifies what happens to our assets when we die, dying is an involuntary act (if it is an 'act' at all), whereas divorcing is fully voluntary (and *is* an act – something we make happen, not something that happens to us). Borrowing the term that has just been introduced, prenuptial agreements reduce the 'commitment of constraint' even further. Constraints that might help to prevent the dissolution of the marriage when it runs into difficulties are removed, or at least weakened, and so the resolve to stay together 'for better, for worse' is already damaged. And that's not all. The motivation behind prenuptial agreements (like most motives) can be ambiguous, even sinister. It can be about control, about using the law to dominate and impose one's will upon one's partner in advance.

Conflict-resolution

We have already taken on board that without good communication, the unity of a marriage is going to be imperilled. A simple technique that may help to deal with conflict (not just in marriages) is the 'Speaker/Listener Technique'. I learned about this at a training day for PREP counsellors (see below), and there are several similar techniques that you are likely to come across. The heart of the technique involves you letting your partner speak freely, while you listen and then summarize what s/he has just said. It is worth practising and acquiring. If you don't use it, or something like it, you may lack an important 'tool' for resolving conflict. That said, mastery of the technique does not guarantee conflicts will be resolved. Beneath our communication skills there must be a deeper commitment that springs from mutual devotion to one another. When this is in place there will already be right motivation to give one's beloved space to speak, to be heard, and understood.

Children

I have included children in this chapter on preparing for marriage because you will need to have discussed what you each think about having them before you marry. Even though the desire to have children may increase as you get older, it is right to state your view now about having children, even if it changes. Differing or opposing expectations about raising a family before marriage are likely to cause conflict later on, and so are children themselves, if and when they arrive, for very many adjustments, concessions and 'sacrifices' will need to be made. If you are already pregnant and deciding to marry, you are declaring the commitment to your child that s/he deserves in order to be loved, accepted and nurtured.

The first thing to say about wanting or not wanting children is that you are likely to have them anyway. Couples who have sexual intercourse often get pregnant! Reliable contraception is only 98 per cent effective, and the longer you use contraception the more likely you are to be in the 2 per cent who become pregnant 'against the odds'. The use of contraception cannot by itself guarantee that any wish not to have children can be carried out. I have read somewhere that every sexually active woman in the USA has 1.8 contraceptive failures in her lifetime. There are very serious issues to consider if you were to use abortion in effect as a back-up contraceptive. That is a very grave (a 'mortal') sin for Roman Catholics. Protestant churches generally allow abortion in exceptional circumstances, but contraception and abortion are very different. Contraception is 'contra-conception' – it is supposed to prevent the creation of a life. Abortion destroys a life already begun. So questions surrounding children really are crucial in testing whether you have a vocation to marriage. Would your present partner be a life-long, devoted parent to any child you conceived together? If not, perhaps you should not even be sleeping with them – still less thinking of becoming married.

We have seen how having children was a principal justification for marriage, and how in the *Common Worship* Preface marriage is differently defined as 'the foundation of family life in which children are [born and] nurtured'. There is no *obligation* to seek to have children. Only the Roman Catholic Church now teaches (and many Roman Catholics simply disregard it) that contraception (but not 'natural family planning')[16] is religiously and morally wrong. The current, official teaching of that church is that there are two purposes of marriage, the good of the partners (the 'unitive purpose') and the conceiving and raising of children (the 'procreative purpose'), and these goods govern every act of sexual intercourse. As the *Catechism* explains:

> The spouses' union achieves the twofold end of marriage: the good of the spouses themselves, and the transmission of life. These two meanings or values of marriage cannot be separated without altering the couple's spiritual life and compromising the goods of marriage and the future of the family.
>
> The conjugal love of man and woman thus stands under the twofold obligation of fidelity and fecundity.[17]

On this view the prevention of conception defies one of God's purposes for marriage, and the separation of the pleasure of love-making from its possible consequence of conception is thought to be spiritually dangerous. But most non-Roman Catholics (and members of the Orthodox churches of the East) disagree strongly with this view. They say that *the marriage itself*, and not every act of sexual intercourse, should be open to the possibility of conception. However, even this view, that there is an obligation to have children (provided the couple are capable of having them) at some stage during the marriage, has receded, and the choice is now left entirely to the couple.

Perhaps the Protestant churches have reached this position because children are likely to come along whatever churches say about having or not having or postponing having them. But there is another fairly big issue to take on directly, and the disagreement between Protestant and Roman Catholic about contraception is partly about this as well. Isn't there a veritable web of social attitudes that are frankly anti-children? And don't we have to ask whether we have got caught up in these without even considering or recognizing them? There are people who feel it is more rewarding to pursue a career than to be a father or mother. But it is possible this attitude places too much value on work and ignores the tremendous satisfaction that being a parent can bring. Some people want to avoid children because of the obvious disruption to the home, including the noise, dirt and smell that they bring. It is possible such people are simply 'house-proud' and really do prefer things to people. Or again, children can be an economic burden, threatening an affluent lifestyle, or an unnecessary curtailment of a hectic social life. The question to be asked here is whether there exists in many societies an inordinate individualism which, frankly, issues in selfishness, and threatens to impair all mutual relationships because one's own interests and preferences are maintained at the expense of others. The desire to avoid children at least requires some forthright self-analysis. There may also be good personal reasons why children are not wanted, perhaps to do with one's own childhood and/or low self-esteem. Even here, though, the feelings we may never yet have articulated should come to the surface and be shared now with our partners. There can be real joy in motherhood and fatherhood that outweighs the personal, social, work-related and economic costs. We are already having fewer children than ever before, and the consequences of not having them include the closure of schools and the undermining of the pensions industry.

There may also be gender problems lurking beneath the desire to refrain from having children. There may be a model, or models, of masculinity which influence young men more than they realize. The desire for personal autonomy, to be ever 'on the move', to be a consumer of everything advanced societies seem to be able to offer – fast cars, sporting and leisure pursuits, alcohol and other social drugs, even women – may militate against the long-term commitment a baby needs if s/he is to be nurtured through childhood and adolescence into adulthood. I once heard a male family therapist say, coarsely but wisely, 'Every man has a dick, but only a real man can raise his children!'[18] There is a recognizable model of maleness that assigns parenthood to mothers and that cops out of responsibility for children that have nonetheless been enthusiastically conceived. It should be exposed.

Career

The fifth 'C' is 'career'. It is increasingly common for women to succeed at further and higher education and consequently to enjoy at least the earning power of men (this is not to concede that there is yet equal pay for men and women who do the same jobs). Employers often expect too much from their employees – that they should move around the country, work unsocial hours, take short holidays, take work home, and increase their productivity year on year. Much of this makes the maintenance of married and family life difficult. Presumably no one today mourns the passing of the days when a wife expected to be 'kept' (and so controlled) by her husband. At the same time it is increasingly necessary for husband and wife to undertake paid work, not least to acquire affordable housing. It is possible to prepare mutually and equitably for this but problems arise when undiscussed assumptions about the careers of each are forced into the open. In order to secure the promotion of one spouse, the other may have to move and jeopardize or suspend his or her career. Are plans shared and jointly owned?

And a sixth 'C'? – church

'Mixed' or 'inter-church' marriages were once also a potential source of friction for couples and their families, but in countries like Britain where only about 10 per cent of people attend a place of worship with any regularity, the different Christian backgrounds or denominations of a married couple are unlikely to be much of a problem. The danger is that in the search for a common 'spiritual home' both partners will forsake their own church backgrounds and stop going. In the USA, where about 40 per cent of citizens attend places of worship, the problem of mixed marriages is much greater. Extensive research done there on 'inter-church couples' concluded that they are

> most at risk for drift from church belonging and practice, and lower expectations of the value of marriage preparation. They leave it with a significant positive shift in attitude, indicating that marriage preparation has served them well, and yet they drift further away from the Church.[19]

Suppose that one or both of you does not profess the Christian faith at all, but for sound reasons you still want to be married in church? What are the clergy likely to make of your application? Generally they will be pleased to provide you with the service you request, provided it would not be contrary to law to do so, *and it is the first marriage for both of you*. Most churches regard baptism as an important (but not the only) criterion of whether a person is a Christian, but let us assume that not even this is true in your own case. As a general rule baptism is not necessary to receive a Christian wedding: 'Any person of British nationality who normally resides in England is entitled to marry in his or her Church of England parish church ... This entitlement applies irrespective of whether either of the couple normally attends church and irrespective of whether either of them has been baptised.'[20] (More about the legal side of marriage in Chapter 5.) A similar welcome awaits you at Nonconformist or Free Churches, although you can expect that the meaning of a church service will be explained to you (the minister might even use this book for the purpose).

Problems used to arise when a Roman Catholic married a baptized Anglican or Protestant Christian, but Roman Catholic teaching on this matter is now permissive. There is a useful website and journal for 'inter-church families',[21] well worth looking at. However, the Roman Catholic spouse usually requires permission to marry a non-Roman Catholic, and this is obtainable from the local priest. He will want to see you both and ensure that according to the Canon Law (Canon 1125) of his church, the Roman Catholic party promises 'to do what you can within the unity of your partnership to have all the children of your marriage baptised and brought up in the Catholic faith'. However, 'the Catholic faith' is understood by Protestants to be broader than the Roman Catholic faith. The Roman Catholic Church acknowledges this and also says that 'the religious upbringing of the children is the joint responsibility of both parents. The obligations of the Catholic party do not, and cannot, cancel out, or in any call into question, the conscientious duty of the other party.'[22] So, decisions about the religious upbringing of your children belong to both of you – no one else. If the marriage is in the Protestant church, the Roman Catholic will need something called a 'dispensation from Canonical form' also obtainable from the priest (or more precisely through the priest but from his bishop). If the marriage is between a Roman Catholic and an unbaptized person, the Roman Catholic Church regards this as an 'impediment' to the marriage, but may grant you a dispensation from the impediment anyway. The Roman Catholic *Catechism* says 'This permission or dispensation presupposes that both parties know and do not exclude the essential ends and properties of marriage and the obligations assumed by the Catholic party concerning the baptism and education of the children in the Catholic Church.'[23] In a mixed marriage you should consult your local clergy from each church at an early stage (not least because any permissions may take months to obtain), and decide with them in which of the two churches you want the marriage to take place.

The most interesting mixed marriages are inter-*religious*, or inter-*faith* marriages where, say, a Christian marries a Jewish or Hindu partner. A series of helpful essays and information about possible benefits and difficulties of inter-faith marriages is available at www.religioustolerance.org.[24] You should talk to representatives of both your faiths, and seek their advice about the possibility of a joint ceremony. Any such ceremony has to fulfil the requirements of civil law and the canon law of the churches. Another alternative is to arrange a civil marriage, and have in addition a religious ceremony or ceremonies afterwards. Interfaith marriages are not immune from difficulties, but they can also provide great richness as the heritage of each tradition represented in the marriage is explored. Disagreements between, say, a liberal or 'mainstream' Jew and a liberal Christian are likely to be less than disagreements between conservative and liberal members of the same faith.

It is also necessary to warn against the extreme views of some churches and religious groups. Religious fundamentalism (where sacred texts are interpreted literally as the words or Word of God) can sanction harmful and offensive views about race, gender and sexual orientation, and it is possible to become involved with these (perhaps seduced by their apparent friendliness, sincerity or enthusiasm) without becoming aware of the full horror of some of their views. As in all things concerning marriage, you should discuss your religious beliefs, and your practice of them, with your partner. Faith should be an important source of richness for your marriage (more on this in Chapter 6). It would be sad indeed if instead it divided you.

Premarital inventories: what they are and whether to use them

Premarital inventories are aids to undertaking the self-examination, mutual discussion and exploration that are needed before you tie the knot publicly. They are much more widely used in the USA (where there is much public concern about the number of marriages ending in divorce) than in the UK, but they are quickly becoming accepted here. We are going to examine two of these briefly.

FOCCUS

FOCCUS stands for Facilitating Open Couple Communication, Understanding and Study. You can reach it at www.foccusinc.com. A good description of what it is and what it does is available on the Scottish Marriage Care website, www.scottish marriagecare.org.uk. Use of FOCCUS is claimed to produce quite startling results in the reduction of divorce and separation, and is described as 'a relationship inventory for couples who are planning to marry. Reflecting current knowledge about the key elements of a successful marriage, FOCCUS helps couples learn more about themselves and their relationship.' How? Let's let the FOCCUS blurb in Scottish Marriage Care speak for itself:

Each partner is asked to read and respond to a number of statements. There are 156 statements in the basic inventory and a number of others geared towards specific issues such as second marriages or inter-faith relationships.

The responses, combined with some biographical information about each partner, are computer-processed to produce a relationship inventory report. Using the report, the Scottish Marriage Care facilitator works with the couple to look at patterns in their responses, discuss issues, and raise awareness of important relationship topics.

The Foccus inventory highlights key problem indicators as well as areas of success in the relationship. It is not a pass or fail test, nor it is a predictor of success or failure in marriage. It aims to identify issues for couples to discuss and work through before marriage.

Occasionally the couple may decide to make a referral for relationship counselling in order to address further the issues raised.

Topic areas covered include: life-style expectations; friends and interests; personality match; personal issues; communication; problem-solving; religion and values; parenting issues; extended family issues; sexual issues; financial issues; readiness issues; marriage covenant; family of origin; dual careers.

For the price of a good meal out (£40) you can buy the full service FOCCUS provides. You will have noticed the mention of a facilitator. FOCCUS is not a DIY kit. The results of your responses may raise questions (about compatibility, for instance) that a trained person will be better placed to interpret. That is why FOCCUS is often encountered as part of a marriage preparation course, including those run by the churches. FOCCUS is recommended by, among others, Marriage Care in England and Wales (www.marriagecare.org.uk)[25] and Marriage Resource (www.marriageresource.org.uk).[26] Marriage Care is in origin a Roman Catholic charity which is now open to everyone, Catholic, Protestant and people of no religious allegiance. Marriage Care uses FOCCUS in courses in some of its 64 centres in the UK (see the on-line directory for details). Marriage Resource has produced a home-video course which you can do on your own (called *Time for Each Other*, cost £31). Marriage Care offers a marriage preparation course that is conducted in cooperation with local churches, so it is well worth finding out if there is one in your area. It says its 'primary concern is for the well-being of the couple', and that it is 'interested in a good celebration of marriage – of making public a private commitment – and of ensuring that the two people involved both know and trust that this person is the one with whom they want to share their life'. Its vision is well expressed on its website:

The route towards certainty requires couples to be aware of the people, events and influences which have helped to shape their life so far. It also means acknowledging the person they have become as a result. As well as being clear about their experience of marriage through their family of origin, people are encouraged to recognise the quality of friendship and intimacy that they share as a couple.

Most couples sense intuitively their sexual and emotional compatibility. What marriage preparation does is shine a light on the partnership tasks which they will be signing up to in marriage. Marriage preparation allows couples to explore safely those tasks in a confidential and secure environment.

For many people the move towards commitment means a considerable shift in mindset which taps naturally into their spirituality. Acknowledgement of this is another aspect of marriage preparation.

PREPARE/ENRICH

Marriage Resource also recommends couples use the PREPARE/ENRICH programme (www.lifeinnovation.com). The aim of the programmes is to help couples prepare for marriage (PREPARE) and to enrich the marriage of those already married (ENRICH). In the USA over a million people have taken the programmes, and they are also available in England (click on International Offices for full contact details). Great success is claimed for these programmes. Like FOCCUS, you have to work with a trained counsellor. First you each separately complete one of five inventories, PREPARE, PREPARE-CC (if you are living together already), PREPARE-MC (if you are married), ENRICH (if you have been married for two years or more), or MATE (if you are married and over fifty). These assess your present relationship. (It is important not to collaborate with your partner when you do this.)

Next you send the inventories away, and the results are summarized into a fifteen-page computer report. The report goes in the first instance to your counsellor. Finally you meet with her or him for between three and six sessions to discuss the report and the issues it raises. You get a workbook, *Building a Strong Marriage*, and you complete six 'couple exercises'. The areas covered are 'sharing strength and growth areas', 'assertiveness and active listening', 'ten steps for resolving conflict', your 'couple and family map', 'financial plans and budget', and your 'goals' as separate persons, as a couple and as a family. The programmes provide for a concentrated focus on potential problems in your marriage, and for space either to confront them or even to proceed no further. If as a result of taking a marital inventory you decided not to proceed to marriage, that would be time and money well spent, wouldn't it?

PREPARE/ENRICH should not be confused with PREP (Prevention and Relationship Enhancement Program) and

C-PREP (Christian PREP). Both of these can be found at www. prepinc.com.[27] PREP rightly calls itself 'one of the most comprehensive and well-respected divorce-prevention/marriage enhancing programs in the world'. There is a substantial essay on the website about C-PREP. The programme 'seeks to lead couples to a model of marriage characterized by respect, sacrifice, commitment, love, and peace: the very things Christ emphasized'. When I visited the website there was no trained instructor in England (but that will change). Another well-known inventory is offered by RELATE (www.byu.edu).[28] A recent RELATE leaflet says:

> Dating, engaged, and married couples can learn about their specific relationships by completing RELATE, a convenient assessment instrument that can be taken without professional assistance. Soon after the questionnaire has been completed, the couple receives a comprehensive RELATE report. Respondents learn about themselves and their partners by reviewing the graphs and charts produced by the RELATE report. The RELATE report also provides the couple with discussion topics and discussion strategies to aid them in their assessment of their relationship.

Some couples will not welcome the soul-searching and attention to detail that the more demanding inventories will require of them. The main point about inventories is that they get you both thinking about issues that are likely to be important to you. There is a list of these (and much else of interest) on the www.2-in-2-1.co.uk/ website.[29] You will not have to agree about everything with your partner, but it is important to agree with each other about what you are disagreeing about! If you come to realize there are major divergences between you about say, money, having children or career, or you become aware your partner has character traits which might make living with him or her difficult, you may want to withdraw from making the unconditional commitment that marriage requires or undertake further work before you proceed any further. Remember the *Common Worship* preface said no one should enter into marriage lightly or selfishly. We should not take for granted that we have a 'vocation' to marriage, or to marriage to this particular person. If we have, it will become evident to us soon enough.

Notes

1. Social Research Unit, University of Surrey Roehampton for the Church of England Diocese of Guildford (March 2002), *Marriage and Adult Relationship Support in Southern England*, sections 3.9 (p. 23) and 3.28 (p. 33). The one in three ratio was in the Church of England (which performs a majority of the marriages).

2. House of Bishops of the General Synod of the Church of England (1991), *Issues in Human Sexuality*. London: Church House Publishing, sections 3.10 and 3.11, pp. 22–3.

3. For strong, supporting evidence see Gill, R. (1999), *Churchgoing and Christian Ethics*. Cambridge: Cambridge University Press.

4. Accessed 28 October 2002.

5. Center for Marriage and Family, Creighton University, Omaha (2000), *Time, Sex, and Money: The First Five Years of Marriage*. For a description of this, and other excellent publications on marriage (from a Roman Catholic perspective), visit www.creighton.edu/MarriageandFamily

6. *The Christian PREP® One-Day Workshop Leader Manual*. Denver, CO: (2000), pp. 47–50.

7. *The Christian PREP® One-Day Workshop Leader Manual*, p. 48.

8. Gray, J. (1993), *Men are from Mars, Women are from Venus: A Practical Guide for Improving Communications and Getting What you Want in your Relationships*. London: Thorsons, p. 31.

9. Dominian, J. (2001), *Let's Make Love: The Meaning of Sexual Intercourse*. London: Darton, Longman & Todd, p. 67.

10. Dominian, *Let's Make Love*, p. 64.

11. 1 John 4.8, 16.

12. *marriage: a teaching document from the House of Bishops of the Church of England*. London: Church House Publishing (1999), p. 7.

13. Dominian, *Let's Make Love*, p. 66.

14. The distinction probably originates in Stanley, S. M. and Markman, H. J. (1992), 'Assessing commitment in personal relationships', *Journal of Marriage and the Family*, 54: 595–608.
15. www.USLaw.com. Accessed 28 October 2002. Most of the websites for prenuptial agreements are currently North American, but similar principles operate in British law.
16. If properly practised, 'natural family planning' is 98 per cent effective. See the handbook, Kippley, J. F. and Kippley, S. K. (1997), *The Art of Natural Family Planning* (4th edn). Cincinnati, OH: Couple-to-Couple League International.
17. *Catechism*, para. 2363, p. 506.
18. In a lecture by Dr Frank Pittman, at the Smart Marriages Conference, Orlando, FL, June 2001.
19. Center for Marriage and Family, Creighton University, Omaha (1995), *Marriage Preparation in the Catholic Church*, p. 47.
20. 'Notes on Marriage in the Church of England', 1.8, 'Entitlement to Marry'. Available at www.cofe.org/lifechanges/index.html. Accessed 29 October 2002.
21. www.aifw.org. Accessed 30 October 2002.
22. These words are taken from the Irish Roman Catholic Bishops' Directory on Mixed Marriages (1983), quoted from the inter-church marriage website www.marriagecouncil.ireland.anglican.org Accessed 30 October 2002. Similar interpretations apply in other countries.
23. *Catechism*, para. 1635, p. 366.
24. Accessed 30 October 2002.
25. Accessed 31 October 2002.
26. Accessed 31 October 2002.
27. Accessed 31 October 2002.
28. Accessed 01 November 2002.
29. Accessed 19 December 2002.

4

Sex, Engagement and Marriage

It always comes as something of a surprise to people outside the churches to learn the official Christian teaching about sex before marriage. The teaching seems clear enough. Sexual intercourse belongs within, and only within, marriage. Outside marriage it is wrong, that is, it is a sin; before marriage, it is the sin of fornication. If you are aware of this teaching you may already feel uneasy about the response you may get from your local priest when you approach him or her to conduct your wedding. You are likely to be among the 70 per cent of couples who live together before they marry, and very likely to be among the 99+ per cent who are sexually experienced before the wedding. In a major survey of sexual behaviour in Britain published in 1994 it was discovered that 'fewer than 1 per cent of men and women aged 16 to 24 were married at the time of their first sexual intercourse'.[1] Are we going to be asked about our sex lives and our domestic arrangements? Are we in for a moral lecture if the priest finds out? In this chapter we will look at the official teaching of the churches about sexual intercourse, the reasons for it, the advantages of it, and the difficulties it faces. Second, we will sketch out an alternative but deeply Christian way of thinking about 'sex before marriage'. Finally living and growing together as an engaged, then a married couple, is compared with the metaphor of a journey – 'the marital journey'. The journey starts earlier than the wedding and reconnects the growing intimacy before the wedding with the growing together that will become the marriage.

Sex before marriage?

The traditional teaching of all the different branches of the Christian Church – Roman Catholic, Anglican, Protestant and Orthodox – is that you must not have sex until you are married. The *Catechism* expresses well the traditional and official view:

> Those who are *engaged to marry* are called to live chastity in continence. They should see in this time of testing a discovery of mutual respect, an apprenticeship in fidelity and the hope of receiving one another from God. They should reserve for marriage the expressions of affection that belong to married love.[2]

Very few practising Christians uphold this teaching, but some do. The Anglican bishops candidly admit the problem: they recognize that most people who marry are sexually experienced, and they do not want to appear to censure them or to widen the gap between the sexually experienced but not-yet-married person and traditional Christian teaching. On the other hand, they want to support young Christians who sincerely believe that it is not simply better but that it is actually the will of God (no less), that they should not have sex until they marry. That is why the bishops say:

> God's perfect will for married people is chastity before marriage, and then a lifelong relationship of fidelity and mutual sharing at all levels. We recognise that it is increasingly hard today for the unmarried generally, and for young people facing peer pressure in particular, to hold to this ideal, and therefore both the Church and its individual members need to be clearer and stronger in supporting those who are struggling against the tide of changing sexual standards.[3]

This task is, however, very difficult. That is why the bishops go on to say: 'we need to give this support in such a way that those who may eventually go with that tide will not feel that in the Church's eyes they are from then on simply failures for whom there is neither place nor love in the Christian community'.

OK to be different?

Many people today find this teaching not only strange but downright unacceptable, even dangerous. A moving story is told of how a Christian couple successfully waited until marriage before they had sex. When she realized after the wedding the extent of his passion for her, and how her personal space was being violated by his constant albeit tender affections, she realized too late that the marriage had been a mistake.[4] Earlier intimacy might have sorted this out before the wedding or led to its cancellation. However, before drawing attention to some of the difficulties with the official view (and how modifications to it can, in fact, quite easily be made), let us think of some *advantages* of the official teaching, even if it is initially difficult to view it positively. I can think of at least three, and there are probably several others.

First, if you don't have sex before you marry you are not going to get pregnant before you both want to be. You won't be worried about contraceptive failure because you won't be using any. This is a big advantage. One of the greatest teachers of the church reckoned the reason why the sin of 'fornication' (sex between unmarried people) was a sin was because it disadvantaged any child who was conceived as a result of it.[5] Of course you can always marry if you are pregnant first, but is it not better for you and your partner to be committed to each other and to any children you may have, *before* you take a pregnancy test?

Second, not having sex with someone you love may encourage the practice of restraint, and restraint is a very useful virtue to have acquired for when you are married. But the practice of restraint is bloody difficult. And that is precisely the point. We all live at a time when our desire for all kinds of things is endlessly and artificially stimulated, when we don't want to wait for anything that we can have immediately, and when the apparent satisfaction of desire is regarded as the supreme good. But the sex drive, or libido, can be strong; indeed for many women and men *immensely* strong. And in turn that means we are going to need a lot of self-control in being faithful to our spouse over the long course of the marriage. And this power of restraint ('continence' it used to be called) is something that can't be taken for granted. It may need to be acquired. 'Constraint' and 'restraint' are very similar terms and we have already seen how our culture has weakened what was called 'the commitment of constraint'; and in those circumstances more emphasis inevitably has to be placed on the single-minded devotion of married partners to each other, without qualification.

Third, Christians have often wanted to witness to the world by presenting to it an alternative way of living. They have a witness to make about sex too. Lack of sexual restraint may lead to great unhappiness, risk to health through sexually transmitted diseases, unwanted children, and (while it may not be noticed at the time) the acquisition of a moral character that becomes unable to be committed for any length of time to another person because it is habituated to separation at the first sign of conflict. That is one of the dangers of living together.[6] So there can be something positive about refraining from sex when you want it that is not based simply on fear of consequences. And there are other reasons. You might think that sex at its best requires self-surrender and self-disclosure at such a deep and vulnerable level, that it should not be undertaken at all unless it is with someone who is deeply and irrevocably committed to you. If you do think this, your thinking coincides with the very best of Christian thought about sex.

Perhaps the common misuse of the sexual freedom acquired during and since the 1960s might prompt the living out of alternative but positive life styles that confront society with its trivialization of sex. Would it not be very worthwhile to contribute to this 'counter-cultural' movement in your own life? If it was once 'cool' for young people to identify themselves as 'alternative' in relation to 'mainstream' behaviour and practice, then nothing could be quite so cool and alternative as not having sex when everyone else is, and not having it for sound reasons.

The case for revision

I have tried to commend the churches' teaching about sex before marriage, and I think there is much to commend it. However, it is not in the main adhered to, and I do not think it is likely to make a comeback in the foreseeable future. Clergy, of all people, are aware of this (even if they are scarcely happy about it). Let's consider why this teaching is widely disregarded, even by Christians themselves, and why the churches have been forced on to the back foot in responding to it. Explanations are easy (and regularly written about). High on the list is the availability of cheap, reliable contraception. For the last 40 years, the contraceptive pill has separated the pleasure of sexual intercourse from a predictable consequence of it – babies. Whatever moral view is taken about contraceptives, they are not going to be 'disinvented' (a bit like nuclear weapons!), so the temptation to use them (again a bit like nuclear weapons!) will always be there.

Second, the comparatively late age of men and women at the time of their first marriages makes sexual experience before marriage practically inevitable. There are good social explanations why people are marrying later. For most of Christian history it was permissible for young men to marry at fourteen, and young women at twelve (this is not to suggest that everyone did in fact get married at these early ages, especially the men): indeed they could become engaged as early as seven. In these circumstances it was much easier to insist on virginity before the wedding. Only in the modern period has going to school become a possibility and then a requirement for all children. The extension of the school-leaving age and the necessity for most young people to go on to further or higher education means that young people are in their twenties, sometimes their late twenties, before they are regarded as qualified for their first career or professional employment. And here there is a real snag in the traditional teaching of the churches – one they have not really come to terms with at all. All churches teach that celibacy is a rare gift, so rare in fact that only the Roman Catholic Church insists that its priests should exercise it. So the churches are saying that you shouldn't have sex until you are married. But they are also saying that you won't have the power of restraint (celibacy) to enable you to avoid having it. And they are also saying that, if you *do* have the gift of celibacy you won't want or need to be married anyway! To say the least, this is a difficult problem for the churches to address.

Third, the mixing of the sexes is a *fait accompli* unthinkable a century ago. Then, if you went out on a date and you belonged to the aristocratic, middle, or upper-middle class, a chaperone would have gone with you! 'Courtship' would be formally conducted under the wary eyes of parents. Schools and colleges are now in the main 'de-segregated'. Men and women mingle together in the armed forces. Since most of the jobs formerly done by men are now open to women, the workplace has become an important space for romantic encounter. Single-sex halls of residence in universities have been phased out in the last 30 years, and cars, mobile phones and e-mail enable personal contacts to be continued from most parts of the globe. The point is that previous generations ingeniously erected barriers that impeded communication between the sexes. Not only have these now been removed but new forms of communication have arrived which make contact ever easier.

Fourth, relative affluence brings the purchase of cars, fashionable clothes, alcohol and Mediterranean holidays within reach of a majority of people. Fifth, the economic independence of women from men removes from them the necessity of seeking a husband or ending up in uncertain spinsterhood. These and many other factors, not least the weakening of the power of religious faith to influence people's personal lives, led to a sexual revolution that had to happen. I think there are enormous benefits from this revolution, but there are also enormous costs, for the weakening of marriage is in no one's interests, and, as we have seen, it undermines the common good.

That is why it is difficult to say quite how you will be received by a priest or minister if you identify as already living with your partner (a common address will give you away!). Clergy won't generally interrogate you about your sex lives, so if you are already having sex with your partner, they are hardly likely to find out about it. I have known ministers who refuse to perform the ceremony for any couple living together unless they separate immediately. But these ministers are likely to belong to very conservative 'free', or 'charismatic' churches, and there are also ministers in these same churches who take a different, much more tolerant, view. A Roman Catholic priest may make plain his church's teaching about cohabitation, but he is unlikely to censure you if you have broken this teaching. Indeed he is likely to be pleased that you are coming to the church for your wedding. You will in any case be required to undertake marriage preparation before marriage in the Roman Catholic Church. Anglican priests belong to a tradition that welcomes allcomers, provided they can be legally married (see Chapter 5). For this reason they know very well that the process of beginning marriage has always been more complicated than the expectation that bride and groom would both be virgins as they stand before the altar.

In my studies of marriage over the last ten years I have been particularly struck by the difference between the way people from (roughly) the end of the eighteenth century onwards think about beginning marriage, and the way it was thought about before that. Prior to that there is a strong case to be made for the view that the entry into marriage was more gradual, going through different phases, and these phases allowed the couple to cope better with the messy in-between period between singleness and 'the point of no return' – the wedding vows. I think there is considerable overlap between the experience of people in the third millennium who become married after they are intimately acquainted with other (and may have lived together) and people who began their marriage as soon as they got engaged. We are going to explore this idea next. My aim will be to suggest that if you have lived together or had sex together first, you are not as far from sound Christian thought and practice as some people believe. Rather, the churches' teaching has some catching up to do.

Engagement and betrothal

Are you 'engaged' yet? Did you have an engagement party? Did you seek the permission of your fiancée's parents to marry her first? Perhaps you didn't think engagement was worth bothering with? What do you think engagement is, or was? What, if anything, does it do?

Well, it seems that no one knows what it does. I looked through a range of books on the subject, and different writers said different things. One said it was a time for increasing acquaintance between the parties; another said it was a 'period of final adjustment'; another said it was an opportunity for couples to decide whether they are in love with each other, and not just 'in love with love'; another thought it was about testing compatibility, or becoming sure about the decision to marry.[7] Other explanations include a period of reflection, a period of preparation, and a period for everyone else to get used to the changed relationships that the marriage would bring about. I call all these indeterminate (and unconvincing) answers 'engagement drift'.[8] They are a clue to something deeper. Engagement has replaced an older way of becoming married, and this involved not engagement, but betrothal. Your marriage service in church is a combination of two rites that were formerly separate and took place at different times.

When does marriage begin? Before or at the wedding?

If you ask people when they think a marriage begins they are very likely to say 'At the wedding, of course', and look at you strangely. This is because of the long-held and deep-seated belief that it is the exchange of consent, through the vows, that 'makes' the marriage. Before you make the vows you are not married. After you make the vows, you are, and a certificate of marriage can be issued. Lawyers like this story. It provides a simple 'before' and 'after', and an exact point in between. But the church has not always thought this way. There are two traditions regarding the beginning of marriage. The conventional Christian view, assumed throughout the world, is that a marriage begins with a wedding. But an earlier Christian view is that marriage begins with betrothal, followed later by the marriage ceremony. Sexual experience regularly began after betrothal and before the wedding. The churches have a real problem in 'accommodating' the growing practice of couples living together, and I think this earlier view has much to commend it in the twenty-first century. But, be warned! There is plenty in the next few paragraphs that would not please all Christians.

This earlier, and alternative, view says the entry into marriage is a process involving stages, with the wedding marking both the 'solemnization' of life commitments *already* entered into, and the recognition and reception of the changed status of the couple by the community or communities to which each belongs. The earlier name in the Church of England for the marriage service was 'The Solemnization of Matrimony'. If you think about this name, it already suggests that matrimony, or the state of being married, has *already* been entered into. It has to have started in order to be 'solemnized'. Once this possibility is recognized, one of the consequences that will undoubtedly follow is that prenuptial cohabitors (we met them early in Chapter 1) will not be having 'sex before marriage'. 'Before marriage' is a 'misdescription' of the relationship because the marriage has already started. The alternative view, that marriage is entered into in stages, renders superfluous those easy temporal distinctions between 'before' and 'after' provided by the identification of the beginning of a marriage with a wedding.

The alternative tradition is assumed by one of the readings at Christmas services provided by Matthew's Gospel:

This is how the birth of Jesus Christ came about. His mother Mary was betrothed to Joseph; before their marriage she found she was going to have a child through the Holy Spirit. Being a man of principle, and at the same time wanting to save her from exposure, Joseph made up his mind to have the marriage contract quietly set aside. (Matthew 1:18–9)

These verses posed a dilemma that the churches never finally resolved. Mary and Joseph were betrothed, but were they married? It seems not, because Matthew says 'before their marriage' Mary found she was pregnant. But Matthew also says Joseph was going 'to have the marriage contract quietly set aside'. The Authorized (1611) Version of the Bible says Joseph, 'not willing to make her a publick example, was minded to put her away privily'. But why would he need to do this unless they were in some sense already married? But, if so, in what sense? In the sense that they were at an intermediate stage in their relationship: no longer single, yet not irrevocably committed to each other because (to use a word from a different period), their marriage had not been 'solemnized'.

Let's dig into a bit of history to make this clearer. In the twelfth century the Western church developed two rival theories of what made a marriage. Gratian (who died in 1159 or a little earlier) and the Italian church held to a two-stage theory of initiation and completion of the marriage. The exchange of consent was the first phase: first intercourse was the consummation.[9] This view combined the old view held in the Roman Empire that marriage was defined by mutual consent, with the newer Christian (and of course Jewish) view that marriage is a 'one flesh' unity of partners. By contrast, Peter Lombard (who died around 1160) and the church in Paris held that consent alone made the marriage. They said this mainly because of what they believed about the marriage of Mary and Joseph. They thought it was a perfect marriage. They also thought that Mary was a virgin, not just when she had Jesus but forever afterwards, a virgin perpetually (*virgo perpetua*). On Gratian's view, they could not have had a perfect marriage because they never had sex. The eventual compromise between these two views was that consent made the marriage (the French view), but first sexual intercourse 'consummated' it (the influence of the Italian view). So if a marriage was not consummated (say through the husband's impotence) it could be dissolved. But once the couple had had sex, the bond was permanent and nothing could break it.

Beginning with betrothal

The importance of the distinction between betrothal and marriage, and the transition from one to the other, cannot be overestimated. The distinction continued until well after the Reformation in the sixteenth century. Up until the sixteenth century, the spousal or spousals 'probably constituted the main part of the contract'.[10] Children conceived during betrothal would be regarded as legitimate, provided the couple married. According to Alan Macfarlane, 'it was really only in the middle of the 16th century that the betrothal, which constituted the real marriage, was joined to the nuptials or celebration of that marriage. Consequently, during the Middle Ages and up to the 18th century it was widely held that sexual cohabitation was permitted after the betrothal.'[11]

In France sexual relations regularly began with betrothal, at least until the sixteenth century when the Roman Catholic Church moved against it.[12] In Britain 'until far down into the eighteenth century the engaged lovers before the nuptials were held to be legally husband and wife. It was common for them to begin living together immediately after the betrothal cere- mony.'[13] According to the social historian John Gillis, 'although the church officially frowned on couples taking themselves as "man and wife" before it had ratified their vows, it had to acknowledge that vows "done rite" were the equivalent of a church wedding'.[14] The term 'processual marriage' is sometimes used to describe these arrangements, 'where the formation of marriage was regarded as a process rather than a clearly defined rite of passage'.[15]

It is no longer generally recognized that the Anglican marriage service was an attempt to combine elements of two separate occasions into a single liturgical event. Macfarlane develops the point in detail:

> In Anglo-Saxon England the 'wedding' was the occasion when the betrothal or pledging of the couple to each other in words of the present tense took place. This was in effect the legally binding act: it was, combined with consummation, the marriage. Later, a public celebration and announcement of the wedding might take place – the 'gift', the 'bridal', or 'nuptials', as it became known. This was the occasion when friends and relatives assembled to feast and to hear the financial details. These two stages remained separate in essence until they were united into one occasion after the Reformation. Thus the modern Anglican wedding service includes both spousals and nuptials.[16]

This 'premodern' distinction between spousals and nuptials has been largely forgotten. Indeed, its very recollection is likely to be resisted by some Christians because it shows a cherished assumption about the entry into marriage – that it necessarily begins with a wedding – to be historically dubious. Betrothal, says Gillis, 'constituted the recognized rite of transition from friends to lovers, conferring on the couple the right to sexual as well as social intimacy'. Betrothal 'granted them freedom to explore any personal faults or incompatibilities that had remained hidden during the earlier, more inhibited phases of courtship and could be disastrous if carried into the indissoluble status of marriage'.[17] It has also been forgotten that about half of all brides in Britain and North America were pregnant at their weddings in the eighteenth century.[18] According to Stone, 'this tells us more about sexual customs than about passionate attachments: sex began at the moment of engagement, and marriage in church came later, often triggered by the pregnancy.'[19] He concludes that 'among the English and American plebs in the last half of the 18th century, almost all brides below the social élite had experienced sexual intercourse with their future husbands before marriage.'

In most churches there was, and in some there still is, some alarm expressed by the spectre of 'sex before marriage'. But it is fairly obvious that what is meant is 'sex before the wedding', and that is a different matter altogether. Were you surprised to read just now that nearly half of all brides were pregnant when they married in the eighteenth century? If you were, that shows how easy it is for society to forget how things once were, and to assume wrongly that things were always as they are now (except that now they are worse!). Stone says that the 'gigantic rise of prenuptial conceptions' (in the eighteenth century) is not 'a massive violation of accepted standards in sexual behaviour', but rather 'a change in those standards'. His judgement is that

In the eighteenth century it looks as if the spousals again became the generally accepted moment at which sexual relations could begin, the marriage ceremony occurring later, often when the bride was quite far advanced in pregnancy. The man's honour was not damaged in the public consciousness, provided that he lived up to his promise to marry despite any possible second thoughts he might subsequently have had; and the woman's honour was not damaged in the public consciousness merely for having commenced sexual relations after the spousals but before the marriage.[20]

Registration by bureaucracy

The Hardwicke Marriage Act of 1753 required registration of all marriages in England and Wales, and set up a bureaucratic apparatus for doing so. Verbal contracts or pledges were no longer regarded as binding. Couples were offered the choice of having banns called (see Chapter 5) in the parish of one of them, or of obtaining a licence to dispense with the banns. Marriages at first took place in parish churches; priests seeking to conduct informal marriages were liable to transportation to America.[21] The creeping extension of government bureaucracy to encompass the entry into marriage is characteristic of the apparatus of the modern nation-state. Uniformity was imposed and policed. Betrothal no longer had any legal force. While the working classes continued to practise alternatives to legal marriage, the stigma of illegitimacy now attached itself to children whose parents had not been through a wedding ceremony. Gone was the transitional phase from singleness to marriage.

The achievement of the widespread belief that a marriage begins with a wedding was not so much a *religious* but a *class* matter. The upper and middle classes had the political clout to enforce the social respectability of the new marriage laws, and they used it. As Gillis writes:

> In the course of the previous hundred years [prior to 1850] both betrothal and wedding had become the subject of passionate controversy, an issue not so much of religion but of class. People in different parts of Britain now married in quite different ways; the distance between the mores of ordinary people and those of the educated élites had never been greater ... From the mid-eighteenth century onwards sexual politics became increasingly bitter as the propertied classes attempted to impose their standards on the rest of society.[22]

New social institutions, like ballrooms and balls, where the sons of gentlemen could initiate romantic attachments, ostentatiously expensive white weddings and 'honeymoons', which separated the couple from their kin as soon as the ceremony had taken place, were all introduced in this period and quickly announced themselves as normative. In the upper class new courtship procedures required the pre-ceremonial virginity of brides, for social rather than for moral reasons. As Gillis explains:

> For all women of this group virginity was obligatory. Their class had broken with the older tradition of betrothal that had offered the couple some measure of premarital conjugality and had substituted for it a highly ritualised courtship that for women began with the 'coming out' party and ended with the elaborate white wedding, symbolizing their purity and status. Couples did not really come to know one another until marriage, a condition that was compensated for by the honeymoon, another of the innovations peculiar to the Victorian upper middle class.[23]

I hope it is by now apparent that the widespread entry into marriage through living together first, at the start of the new millennium, represents remarkable parallels with practice in pre-modern Britain. The 'destigmatization' of pregnancy prior to a wedding is a return to earlier but still modern ways. Even the recent licensing of hotels, casinos and football stadia as places where marriages may be conducted replicates earlier freedoms where wedding vows could be exchanged anywhere. Gillis' verdict, written in 1985, is that

> Together law and society appear to have reinstated a situation very much like that which existed before 1753, when betrothal licensed premarital conjugality. It is also like the situation that existed in the late eighteenth and early nineteenth centuries when so many people made their own private 'little weddings', postponing the public, official event until such time as they could gather the resources necessary to a proper household.[24]

But the conclusion that there are remarkable parallels between premodern times and our own should, however, only be accepted with caution. The 'premarital conjugality' of the earlier period occurred within a theological and social framework that was nonetheless strict with regard to having sex outside marriage. It insisted on marriage as the precondition of raising children, and it fiercely insisted on fathers assuming responsibility for the welfare of the children they helped to conceive 'out of wedlock'. Pre-industrial communities were largely self-regulating, and the full sexual experience practised by betrothed couples was, unlike the practice of couples today living together 'non-nuptially', emphatically premised by the intention to marry. Once a marriage had been contracted it was indissoluble, and divorce, unless you could afford a special Act of Parliament, was unavailable.

The stages of the marital journey

I have suggested that bringing back betrothal would help the churches deal with a big problem for them, i.e., how to deal with people who want a church wedding but who appear to live contrary to church teaching. But all that is incidental – it may take 50 more years to tell whether these arguments are useful to the churches. In the meantime, you are getting married; you are probably living with your partner already and almost certainly having sex with him or her. If in these circumstances you now want a church wedding I don't think you have done anything to deserve censure, and neither probably do you. There is only a hint of censure in the Church of England's teaching document *marriage*, which says:

> The social and emotional steps by which couples come to enter marriage are often complicated, and some finally think about lifelong commitment only when they are already living together. This route of approaching marriage is exposed to uncertainties and tensions and is not to be recommended. But it was not uncommon in earlier periods of history, and the important thing is simply that the point of commitment should be reached.[25]

But it is possible to be a lot more positive (and a lot less tentative) about living together before the ceremony, and this tends to get lost in the discussion. It is exciting to live at a time when the pace of social change is so fast that the churches have failed to keep up with it. Equally in new social situations the wisdom of past generations is still sorely needed. We saw in Chapter 1 that some social changes had ambiguous effects on marriages and children and did not promote the common good. What matters most is that our growing together before the wedding promotes our *own* good *and* the common good, and I am convinced that that can happen. In a short book there is space only for two reflections about this: one about God and one about our 'marital journey'.

Perhaps the most powerful reason for wanting a church wedding is that you rightly want God's blessing on your marriage. The most important belief Christians entertain about God is that 'God is love'. When we looked at the 'C's of communication and commitment in Chapter 2 we noted how the Church of England's 'teaching document' on marriage started with the sentence 'God is love', and how Jack Dominian spoke movingly of love-making as a 'divine language'. In that part of our 'marital journey' where we approach the wedding, make our final decisions about whether to commit for life with our partner, and so on, we are likely to experience new heights and depths of human love. Indeed, the beginnings of that complete commitment which will remain when the novelty and excitement of first love-making grows a little fainter, will also be grounded in this period when we are attracted by the realization that there is more to love than sex. From the point of view of Christian faith, nothing less than a tragedy has occurred in the relationship between the churches and the young people coming to them for marriage.

Tragedy? Yes: that human love which expresses itself in sexual experience and increasingly in coming to live together has become separated from the understanding of divine love, because of the negative attitudes towards it associated with terms such as 'living in sin', 'fornication', and so on. Couples have been unable to make the connection between their love for each other and God's love for them both because they have internalized the negative judgements that they think the churches have made about their sexual conduct and lifestyle. So, just at the time in their lives which is potentially crucial for a religious understanding of self, of love and of God as love, negative judgements about sex sever the vital connection between their sexual and their spiritual lives.

Religious faith is always grounded in some human experience or other. This is because God our Creator communicates with us through God's creatures, through what God in the first place created. How better to understand the love of God than through the intense and escalating love that we encounter with and through the one we want to commit to for ever? Christians think God acts through human actions (although God need not be confined to acting this way). So, if God acts to prevent suffering, it is likely to be through the human actions of building hospitals, becoming doctors and nurses, doing research on HIV, and so on, that God's love for the world gets known. In a similar way God loves through human loving. By your love for your partner and your partner's love for you, God's love reaches you too. The *Common Worship* communion service contains the prayer, 'Give grace to us, our families and friends, and to all our neighbours, that we may serve Christ in one another, and love as he loves us.'[26] There are similar prayers in the communion services of the other churches. The prayer makes our point about the overlapping of divine and human love in a slightly different way. It suggests that we find Christ in one another, and that all human loving is a sharing of the love of Christ for us. Beginning marriage provides an intense personal disclosure of each to the other. What is potentially and fruitfully also a divine disclosure has been sullied and spoilt by the assumption that it is the subject of religious condemnation.

It is clear that many of the social changes that occurred in the previous century have impacted on our personal lives, and one such impact is the lengthening period that it takes to become married. In Britain we take our GCSE exams at about sixteen, often followed by A levels at eighteen. The British government is planning for 50 per cent of young people to experience higher education (education to degree level) and for many more to experience 'further', post-school education in practical and vocational subjects. It commonly takes five years between leaving school and entering a first job or professional career, more if a 'gap year' is grabbed along the way. The price of housing over time rises faster than salaries, so the period before first house purchase is also likely to be extended. It is no wonder that couples are postponing entry into marriage until the late twenties or early thirties. This long and lengthening period between puberty and marriage represents a challenge to the churches' teaching about chastity, and I have suggested how that challenge might be met.

I got married (like most of my friends) at twenty-two, immediately after leaving university. My wife was a year older. We had the benefit of membership of a Baptist church that maintained strict and conventional teaching about 'no sex before marriage'. Christian influence and institutions were stronger then, and the power of the expectation that we would be 'chaste' until we married kept us from having sexual intercourse with each other (although not from much else), but only for a time. Eventually we felt that the traditional teaching that we affirmed with our minds we could no longer uphold with our bodies, and we couldn't stand the split between them. We were sufficiently confident in our faith to remain untroubled by our departure from the strict rule, but we both had to refuse the temptation to internalize the negative reactions that we knew would follow the (unlikely) disclosure of our practice.

Nearly 40 years on, waiting until the age of thirty to become sexually experienced seems not only daunting, but also unnecessary. It also seems that the strict teaching forbidding sex before the wedding (although it was defended earlier in the chapter) fails on several counts. Either it is ignored (in which case ignoring other more important teaching is likely to follow swiftly); or it is accepted for a time (in which case Christian couples may feel overtaken by a sense of failure when the pressures to uphold it are too great), or in a few cases, it is accepted. Even here one cannot be confident that saintliness has been achieved. Waiting too long can be emotionally harmful. (St Paul warned about this in connection with married couples practising abstinence.) Or, as we have seen, important self-knowledge and knowledge of one's partner, relevant to the decision to marry, is withheld.

Another alternative is to marry much earlier in life, and so avoid the lengthy wait. This certainly reduces the tension, but it also increases the likelihood of marital breakdown later, and cannot be generally recommended.

The marital journey for couples in the new century is likely to follow a slightly different path to the same destination. When my fiancée and I were technically unmarried (but completely committed to each other) and having sex, we never knew about the alternative tradition that has been the subject of this chapter. If it was even known about (apart from a few professional social historians) it was a well-kept secret. But knowledge of it would have rendered all the angst associated with the contravention of Christian teaching unnecessary. The fixed point along the path is the nuptials or solemnization. In Christian teaching marriage is for life, and the vows made during the service should not be made without the intention to stay together until death. Couples are increasingly treating nuptials as spousals, that is, treating their weddings as if they were firm commitments, but ones that can still be backed out of for due cause. The nuptials must remain the point in the growing marriage where backing out is, in intention, closed off (more on this in Chapter 7). Working backwards from the nuptials, it is helpful to see the preceding period as the phase when the vocation to marriage is tested, both in general ('Can I, do I want to be faithful to another person for the rest of my life?') and in particular ('Can I, do I want to be faithful to *this* person for the rest of my life?').

The long path to the nuptials, I suggest, might be recognized by another point along the way. This point was once called the spousals, or the beginning of the betrothal period. Whether or not betrothal comes to be reinstated by the churches, and a service offered to mark it out, it may be helpful now to think of it as a point along the way to the irrevocable point when the nuptial vows are made. Like the nuptials proper it is a state that no one should enter 'lightly or selfishly but reverently and responsibly in the sight of almighty God'. It is permissible, and you may think it helpful, to regard that point as the one where your marriage begins, where you are no longer single, but you are not yet at the farther point where your marriage is permanently set in promises to each other before God. This in-between period may be one which offers intense joy as you move towards complete commitment, or, conversely, second thoughts about the permanence that beckons.

Notes

1. Wellings, K., Field, J., Johnson, A. M. and Wadsworth, J. (1994), *Sexual Behaviour in Britain: The National Survey of Sexual Attitudes and Lifestyles.* Harmondsworth: Penguin, p. 72.
2. *Catechism*, para. 2350, p. 503.
3. House of Bishops, *Issues*, p. 22, para. 3.8.
4. Anderson, H. and Fite, R. C. (1993), *Becoming Married.* Louisville, KY: Westminster/John Knox Press, p. 119.
5. Aquinas, T., *Summa Theologiae*, 2a2ae.154.2. In other places, he gives other reasons why fornication is wrong.
6. Thatcher, A. (2002), *Living Together and Christian Ethics.* Cambridge: Cambridge University Press, pp. 25–8.
7. Thatcher, *Living Together*, pp. 204–6.
8. Thatcher, *Living Together*, p. 204.
9. For the background, see Brundage, J. A. (1993), *Sex, Law and Marriage in the Middle Ages.* Aldershot: Variorum, Ashgate Publishing, pp. 407–11; Brooke (1989), *Medieval Idea of Marriage.* Oxford: Clarendon Press, pp. 126–39. For a fuller version of the argument here see Thatcher, A. (1998), 'Beginning marriage: two traditions', in Hayes et al., (eds), *Religion and Sexuality*, pp. 415–26.
10. Macfarlane, A. (1987), *Marriage and Love in England: Modes of Reproduction 1300–1840.* Oxford: Basil Blackwell, p. 291.
11. Macfarlane, *Marriage and Love in England*, p. 305.
12. See Rémy, J. (1979), 'The family: contemporary models and historical perspective', in A. Greeley (ed.), *The Family in Crisis or in Transition: A Sociological and Theological Perspective.* Concilium, 121: New York: Seabury, p. 9.
13. Macfarlane, *Marriage and Love in England*, p. 374.
14. Gillis, J. (1985), *For Better, for Worse: British Marriages, 1600 to the Present.* New York and Oxford: Oxford University Press, p. 20.

15. Parker, S. (1990), Informal Marriage, Cohabitation and the Law, 1750–1989. New York: St Martin's Press, p. 19.
16. Macfarlane, *Marriage and Love in England*, pp. 309–10.
17. Gillis, *For Better, for Worse*, p. 47.
18. Stone, L. (1993), 'Passionate attachments in the West in historical perspective', in K. Scott and M. Warren (eds), *Perspectives on Marriage: A Reader.* New York: Oxford University Press, p. 176. The figure cited here is 'at least half of all brides'. In Stone, L. (1979), *The Family, Sex and Marriage in England 1500–1800.* London: Weidenfeld & Nicolson, the figure is 'over 40 per cent' (p. 609).
19. Stone, 'Passionate attachments', p. 176.
20. Stone, *The Family*, p. 629.
21. Outhwaite, R. B. (1995), *Clandestine Marriage in England, 1500–1800.* London and Rio Grande: Hambledon Press, pp. 84–5.
22. Gillis, *For Better, for Worse*, p. 135.
23. Gillis, *For Better, for Worse*, p. 164.
24. Gillis, *For Better, for Worse*, p. 310.
25. marriage, p. 10.
26. Available online at www.cofe.anglican.org Accessed 14 November 2002.

5

Our Wedding Ceremony

In this chapter we are going to look first at some of the formalities that need to be observed prior to a marriage in church taking place. Most of the chapter is devoted to the ceremony itself. We shall look at the meaning of the different parts of the marriage service and explain some of the choices that the service allows you to make in creating your own 'tailor-made' wedding service.

Preliminaries

This is some simple on-line information that explains the formalities very well. If you marry in a parish church of the Church of England or Church in Wales, it is helpful to go to www.facul tyoffice.org.uk/marriage.html in order to find out about the legal preliminaries to your wedding. On the main Church of England website there is a very helpful section on 'Planning your wedding' and 'Notes on marriage in the Church of England' (www.cofe.anglican.org then click on 'Planning your wedding'). There is also a government leaflet, *Getting Married*, about marrying in a Register Office (you may find it interesting to compare church and state preliminaries) available on-line.[1] It must be said that church and state are both reviewing marriage preliminaries, so this part of the chapter may get out of date rather quickly.

English law governing church weddings distinguishes between the Church of England (which conducts two-thirds of all church weddings in England) and other churches, including Roman Catholic. If your wedding is in a non-Anglican church, you are both required by law to give notice of your intention to marry (the 'notice of marriage') to the local superintendent registrar at the Register Office in the district in which you each live. You must show up personally at the office, together if you live in the same district. If you live in different districts, you must register separately in each district. You must have lived in the district for at least seven days before you register, and there must be sixteen clear days between registration and the wedding. Some of these churches are licensed for the performance of marriages, and clergy may be 'authorized persons' who can perform marriages without the presence of a registrar. In other circumstances a registrar may need to attend the church, chapel, assembly hall, or meeting house in order to register the wedding. The minister or priest of the church where you wish to marry will advise you. Clearly, if you or the minister need to book a registrar, as well as everything else, you should attend early to these formalities.

If your wedding is in an Anglican church, you will need to have your banns 'called' (or 'read', or 'published') (exceptions in a moment). As the 'Notes on Marriage in the Church of England' explain, 'Banns are the public announcement that two people wish to marry, and an invitation to anybody who knows just cause or impediment to the union to declare it.' The calling of the banns is an ancient practice (though it may not be legally required for much longer). It goes back long before proper marriage records were kept, when the only way to detect an impediment to a marriage (for example, if a partner was married already) was to call the banns in each of the parishes and see whether anyone knew of a reason why the couple should not, or legally could not, marry. Each of you needs to live in the parish where your banns are read. There is no minimum number of days you must live there in order to qualify to marry by banns, but your minister will need to be satisfied that your claim to residency there is genuine. So on three Sundays prior to the wedding, the banns are read out in the parish church (or churches) of the future bride and groom. It is very desirable (but not a requirement) that you attend the services at which your banns are read, especially when they are read in the church where your marriage will take place. You will not have to do anything. Sometimes prayers are offered for couples when their banns are published, and if you do not attend the church regularly in which you will be married, you may be encouraged to get a first-hand experience of your local church during these services. One very simple and appropriate prayer goes:

> Lord of love,
> we pray for N and N.
> Be with them in all their preparations
> and on their wedding day.
> Give them your love in their hearts
> throughout their married life together,
> through Jesus Christ our Lord.[2]

Can you, is there any advantage to, marry by obtaining an 'ecclesiastical licence', instead of having your banns called? There are two types of licence, 'common' and 'special'. If you are only a temporary resident in the parish where you will marry, you can still marry there but you will need a common licence from the bishop (sometimes also called the 'Bishop's Licence'). The legal requirement is that at least one of you must be genuinely resident at an address within the parish where the marriage is to take place for a minimum of fifteen days immediately prior to the issuing of the licence. The licence is then valid for three months. The licence is issued on the authority of the Diocesan Bishop, and application is usually made to the official called the 'Bishop's Surrogate for Marriage Licences' in that area (the minister at the church may be the 'surrogate' but, if not, he or she will know who should be contacted). If neither of you can satisfy the fifteen-day residence requirement you may still be able to marry in that parish by obtaining a 'special licence' which is issued on the authority of the Archbishop of Canterbury only. As the 'Planning your wedding' guide explains[3] a special licence is 'only granted in exceptional (special or emergency) circumstances'. An application cannot be considered 'unless the minister at the church in question is prepared both to take the Marriage service and to support the licence application'.[4]

The ceremony

One of your meetings with the vicar or minister is almost certain to be about the content of the marriage service. We are going to have a good look at this next. I hope you are as impressed with it as I am. You may be surprised at the amount of choice you have with regard to the content of your wedding, especially if you use the *Common Worship* marriage service. Don't forget that, if you don't have an Anglican wedding, there is actually little difference among the churches in their beliefs about marriage (but not divorce!), and the services are similar too. You can borrow or buy the booklet, or download the marriage service directly from www.cofe.anglican.org For a detailed discussion of the service (the one that clergy read) get Stephen Lake's *Using Common Worship Marriage*.[5] You can find the wedding ceremonies of the Church of Scotland, the Greek Orthodox Church, the United Reformed Church, the Quakers and the Salvation Army all at www.weddingguideuk.com/articles/cere-monies/ default.asp. There are also details of Hindu, Buddhist, Sikh, Jewish and humanist ceremonies to be found there, and much helpful background reading.

An early decision about the service is whether you also wish to receive holy communion as part of it. If you take communion (are 'communicants') regularly, you will probably wish to have holy communion, or the eucharist, as part of your service. If you do not attend the eucharist regularly, the possibility of holy communion in your service is still worth thinking about. There is nothing more holy in Christian worship than holy communion, and the opportunity to combine your service with communion should not lightly be set aside. That said, a majority of services probably do not have communion, and you will not be expected to include it if you do not want it (for whatever reason). The service with communion is called 'The Marriage Service within a Celebration of Holy Communion' (and can be downloaded from the same website as the other *Common Worship* marriage texts). The service is very similar to 'The Marriage Service', but has a further section, 'The Liturgy of the Sacrament', at the very end.

All about love

The first thing to notice is the loving atmosphere that the liturgy generates. It celebrates God's love for us all, and your love for one another. In the welcome the priest may read the sentence from the Christian scriptures which describes what God is: 'God is love, and those who live in love live in God and God lives in them.' (1 John 4:16). The opening prayer acknowledges that human love has a divine source which is also at the very root of good human action:

God of wonder and of joy:
grace comes from you,
and you alone are the source of life and love.
Without you, we cannot please you;
without your love, our deeds are worth nothing.
Send your Holy Spirit,
and pour into our hearts
that most excellent gift of love ...

In the Preface to the service (we studied this in Chapter 2) the vicar tells the congregation why they have come:

to witness the marriage of *N* and *N*,
to pray for God's blessing on them,
to share their joy
and *to celebrate their love*.[6]

You may recall that the Preface explains how marriage is given

that as man and woman grow together *in love and trust*,
they shall be united with one another in heart, body and mind,
as Christ is united with his bride, the Church.

Another purpose of marriage was that

... each member of the family, in good times and in bad,
may find strength, companionship and comfort,
and *grow to maturity in love*.

You will shortly be asked whether you will *love* your wife or husband to be, and before you make your vows the priest will pray to God,

Pour out your blessings upon N and N,
that they may be joined *in mutual love and companionship*,
in holiness and commitment to each other.

You will promise '*to love* and to cherish' your partner, and your rings will be called 'a symbol of unending *love* and faithfulness'. There are many more references to love in the service, and even more where love is implied. The point to spot is not just that there are many references in the service to you and your partner's love, and God's love. It is that when these references to love are made as the service unfolds around both of you, an atmosphere of love is created that everyone there shares in. This is a beautiful experience, and when combined with the beauty of the clothes (and the people wearing them!), the flowers, the smiles, the church building itself, and the hopes of and for you both, the experience can become almost overpowering. You don't get this in a Register Office!

Choosing the hymns

You can of course choose the hymns, and you can have up to three. The minister remains responsible for the conduct of the service and s/he will advise about whether a particular hymn is suitable. You may have firm favourites that you would want included, but you might be surprised and delighted to discover the wealth of new wedding hymns which also have the advantage of being set to more traditional tunes that some people in the congregation are likely to know. The hymn book that is used at my local church is called *Celebration Hymnal for Everyone* and it contains a modern (1994) collection of more than 850 hymns. But in the back there is an index, in fact several indexes, and one of these, called the 'liturgical index', has a section, 'Marriage', that lists all the hymns in the book that are written or chosen especially to be sung at marriage services.[7] Other modern hymn books provide similar opportunities, well worth exploring. You may want to have an order of service for your wedding printed, with the hymns and other details printed on it. If you reproduce hymns which are modern (i.e., within 70 years of the author's death) the owner of the copyright should be acknowledged on the order of service. (The minister will advise you about this, and s/he will know whether the church has a copyright licence,[8] making your reproduction of copyright hymns free.) The web version of the marriage service actually begins with the structure of the service, naming the different parts of it. This can be very useful if you are making and printing an order of service for your big day.

Some local churches have their own websites with detailed guidance about making appointments with the minister, times and policies about marriage and marriage preparation, and so on. Some even have suggestions about the hymns and the music for weddings. A friend of mine who is at present Vicar of Norton in Letchworth Garden City, and who knew I was writing this book, casually told me there was a section on weddings, including wedding hymns, on his parish website. When I visited www.parishofnorton.org.uk[9] and clicked on 'Baptisms/ Weddings and Funerals', I was astonished at what was available. There are 44 hymns listed as suitable for use at weddings and the text of all of them is only another click away. The tunes that go with some of the hymns are also listed, so if you are uncertain about how they will sound, you can click on the audio file, and download and play it very easily. This site also helps you choose the music that you would like played before, during and after the ceremony. There are nineteen pieces of music for you to sample, including extracts from *The Deer Hunter* and *The Sound of Music*. It is to the great credit of this parish church that it has a website that gets you thinking about the choices available to you regarding your hymns and music. Since the parish encourages visitors, do check it out for yourself. A commercial website, www.webwedding.co.uk[10] also has a 'music maestro' area, with useful suggestions about suitable music.

Any objections?

After the first hymn the priest will say, 'I am required to ask anyone present who knows a reason why these persons may not lawfully marry, to declare it now.' The question will be reminiscent of earlier times when communities were generally smaller and more closely knit, and national registers were not kept. There is always a sense of relief when the short silence after the question is put, is uninterrupted by imagined objectors! In fact, there is little anyone can object to, especially as you will already have obtained the appropriate certificates (or licence) for the minister to agree to hold the wedding in the first place. Unless you are under age, already married, too closely related to your partner, or marrying a 'foreign national' without proper documentation, no one could have anything serious to object *to*.[11] You are then reminded that 'The vows you are about to take are to be made in the presence of God, who is judge of all and knows all the secrets of our hearts', and the same question, first put to the congregation, is put to both of you. If you think it sounds fierce, think of the older Prayer Book version:

> I require and charge you both, as ye will answer at the dreadful day of judgement when the secrets of all hearts shall be disclosed, that if either of you know any impediment, why ye may not be lawfully joined together in Matrimony, ye do now confess it.

In the days when verbal confirmation was the only means of confirming people's identity and eligibility for marriage, great importance was placed upon the assent of the community or communities from which the couple had come, and the reminder about the dreadful day of judgement deliberately put the frighteners on parties who had something to hide. It is perhaps a reminder that telling the truth is still essential to the conduct of civil and religious life.

'I will': the Declarations

Next the minister asks whether you will 'love', 'comfort', 'honour and protect' each other, and 'forsaking all others', be faithful to each other 'as long as you both shall live'. This is the biggest question you will ever answer! It brings together all we were thinking about in Chapter 2 about becoming 'one flesh' and about marriage being a covenant. You will make each other feel very special when you answer 'I will' to this question, because you are saying 'There is, and there will always be, no one else for me.' When you marry in church your faithfulness to each other has an extra ingredient in its mix. The Christian faith celebrates the love of God for the world and the love of Christ for the church. This faithful God underwrites human faithfulness. Your faithfulness to one another can, with God's blessing, become a mirror of God's own faithfulness to us all.

There is a new question in *Common Worship*. The *congregation* then gets asked 'Will you, the families and friends of *N* and *N*, support and uphold them in their marriage now and in the years to come?', and they are supposed to respond, loudly, 'We will.' If the clergyperson briefs them beforehand, a robust response can be readily elicited. I like this addition. It is brief, affirmative and involving. I like to think this new question is influenced by the idea that marriage is a sort of 'commonwealth' (see Chapter 2). When I joined in with everyone else in a forthright 'We will' recently, it prompted the thought that it is everybody's business to support each other in their marriages, because good marriages are necessary in promoting the common good.

There is another point about saying 'I will' that has become so deeply buried in history that everyone has forgotten about it. 'I will' is in the future tense. When we say we will do something we mean we will do it at some time in the future, and we are not going to do it right now. I think 'I will' goes back to the time when people entered marriage by becoming betrothed first, and when they were very obviously making a promise to solemnize their marriage at some time in the future.[12] In Chapter 4 we saw how betrothal made good sense of growing into marriage prior to solemnizing it at the point after which there is no backing out. If the answer 'I will' helps you to think about your marriage as something that is growing and moving towards a deepening commitment, that will be an additional layer of meaning for you to savour when you eventually say it in public.

Choosing the readings

You won't be surprised that there will be a reading or two from the Bible at your ceremony, but did you know you could choose which ones (and the readers)? Click on 'here' in the Readings section of the Marriage Service to view 25 different readings from the Bible in contemporary translation. There are some very well-known ones, including St Paul's famous eulogy about love (1 Corinthians 13), the one about husbands loving their wives as Christ loves the Church (Ephesians 5:21–33), the one that teaches that God is love (1 John 4:7–12) and Jesus's teaching about marriage and children (Mark 10:6–9,13–16) and about happiness ('Blessed are the poor in spirit . . . ' Matthew 5:1–10). My favourites (perhaps I'm biased because my son and daughter-in-law chose them for their wedding in 2001) are a fantastic poem in praise of human love in the Hebrew scriptures (Song of Solomon 2:10–13; 8:6), and the story of Jesus turning water into wine (John 2:1–11). If you are looking for something else, there is a wide selection of appropriate readings, religious, non-religious, and 'in-between' at www.4wed.net/readings.htm.

The Song of Solomon (or 'Song of Songs') is a collection of erotic love songs probably sung at wedding receptions, or hen and stag nights in ancient Israel. For centuries, the translation of the text has not brought out the erotic imagery. Consequently, generations of people have been deprived of the enjoyment of it, and may not even know of its existence or its availability to be included in the marriage service. That is why I have mentioned it here. This is the extract in the *Common Worship* readings list:

> My beloved speaks and says to me:
> 'Arise, my love, my fair one,
> and come away;
> for now the winter is past,
> the rain is over and gone.
> The flowers appear on the earth;
> the time of singing has come,
> and the voice of the turtle dove
> is heard in our land.
> The fig tree puts forth its figs,

and the vines are in blossom;
they give forth fragrance.
Arise, my love, my fair one,
and come away.'

Set me as a seal upon your heart,
as a seal upon your arm;
for love is strong as death,
passion fierce as the grave.
Its flashes are flashes of fire,
a raging flame.
Many waters cannot quench love,
neither can floods drown it.
If one offered for love
all the wealth of one's house,
it would be utterly scorned. (Song of Solomon 2:10–13;
8:6)

All five of the senses are engaged in this poem, even those of
smell and taste. The experience of the senses is worked into the
sense of a new beginning in the cycle of nature, and the love of
the couple is worked into both. The seal is reminiscent of the
wedding ring, and the admission of the strength and depth of
passion between lovers is probably the strongest affirmation
of sexual love in the Bible. The 'raging flame' of passion can also
be translated 'the flame of God', making the connection, in the
Hebrew language, between the couple's passionate love and the
very nature of God.[13]

Giving away the bride?

A note in the written text of the service (but not in the web version) allows for the traditional 'Giving Away' of the bride. In the
old Prayer Book service, immediately after the Declarations,
the minister asks 'Who giveth this Woman to be married to this
Man?' He receives the bride 'at her father's or friend's hands',
and the bridal couple proceed with their vows. *Common Worship*
removes the 'Giving Away' but allows it to be reintroduced as a
(much revised) option, indeed several options.[14] If you choose,

the minister will ask 'Who brings this woman to be married to this man?' At least 'brings' is better than 'gives'. The bride is a woman, not a present or a commodity to be handed over to anyone by anyone. The bride's mother, or another member of the family, may now do the bringing or handing over. Or the bride's father may answer on behalf of himself and the bride's mother, 'My wife and I do.' The Methodist marriage service retains as an option for 'a relative or friend' of the bride, or of both bride and groom, the question 'Who presents C to be married to A?' Another option (clearly to be agreed beforehand) is for the minister to ask both sets of parents:

N and N have declared their intention towards each other.
As their parents,
will you now entrust your son and daughter to one another
as they come to be married?

And the parents can reply: 'We will.'

So there are lots of choices. Let's review them briefly. First, you could ignore the Giving Away altogether, avoiding any implication that the bride is a commodity to be handed over. This is the solution adopted in the main text of *Common Worship*. Its advantage is that it acknowledges that the Giving Away has been, and remains, sexist. The giving or bringing of a woman by one man, to a second man, then to be married to a third man remains the historical form of the Giving Away. One way of removing the sexism of this part of the rite, is to remove the part from the service altogether, along with the sexism that remains undisguised.

Another option, perhaps unlikely to be chosen by readers of this book, is to retain the Giving Away in its traditional form and language. If this appeals to you, you may wish to use for your whole service the old 1662 Prayer Book 'Solemnization of Matrimony' which remains legal in the Anglican Church.

A third option is to retain the Giving Away in a revised form, using 'brings' not 'gives' and involving someone else in addition to (or instead of) the bride's father. This option has the advantage of involving the bride's family, and retaining the old tradition of Giving Away but in a revised form.

The fourth option is to replace the Giving Away with something else (the quotation above does this). There are several advantages to this. It involves *both* the bride's parents. It recognizes that bringing the bride to be married is still sexist (no one brings the groom), and deals with that problem by involving the groom's parents as well. The wording 'entrust . . . to one another' is intended as a strong declaration of parental support for the marriage. A possible disadvantage is that it is too obviously a replacement for something that is increasingly an embarrassment, both to the church and to people who come to the church for marriage. But the fourth option remains popular with parents who welcome increased involvement in the making of the marriage. That's why I think options one or four are much better than two and three. The choice is yours.

'I do': the vows

The vows are at the heart of the service, because the saying of these in the presence of witnesses, is what makes the marriage in Western canon law happen. It is the exchange of consent in the present tense. In grammar the vows are called 'performatives' – words that make things happen merely by saying them. You will each say:

> I, *N*, take you, *N*,
> to be my wife [husband],
> to have and to hold
> from this day forward;
> for better, for worse,
> for richer, for poorer,
> in sickness and in health,
> to love and to cherish,
> till death us do part,
> according to God's holy law.
> In the presence of God I make this vow.

There is a timeless beauty, an elegant simplicity, and a profound depth to these words. That is the reason why they have

changed little from the vows in the 1662 service. They manage
to express, succinctly and exquisitely, the very kernel of the
understanding of marriage in Christianity. 'From this day forward' marks the point of transition from provisional to total
commitment to one another, which the service is. 'For worse' is
the reminder that the commitment made, in intention at least,
is stronger than any difficulty that might come to be waged
against it; 'for poorer' is a reminder that the commitment made,
in intention at least, is stronger than the vagaries of personal
wealth, of economic fortune or misfortune; 'in sickness' is a
reminder that illness is one of the reasons why the pledges we
make to one another in marriage are unconditional; 'to cherish'
is a reminder that passionate and romantic love requires a
deeper form if it is to be maintained throughout the marriage;
'till death us do part' is a reminder that your commitment, while
made in time, transcends time, in that only the death of one of
you can break it.

'Obey'?

There are two alternative forms of the vow you can make. Both
require the wife to vow obedience to her husband. In one, the
line 'to love and to cherish' becomes 'to love, cherish, and obey',
straight from the old Prayer Book vows. The second alternative
is simply the 1662 version of the vows in full. The last two lines
of the vows restores the archaic language: 'according to God's
holy ordinance; and thereto I plight thee my troth'. I can only
welcome the removal of 'and obey' from the main text of the
service. 'Wifely' obedience definitely belongs in one of those old
bottles we talked about in Chapter 2, and the sooner this old
bottle gets smashed the better. This form of the bride's vows is
incompatible with the entire atmosphere of the new service
with its emphasis on love and mutuality. It represents assumptions about the place of women in a male-dominated, patriarchal society, and it associates the church with the oppression of
women. Its retention as an option possibly has the value of hon-
esty – yes, the tradition really did require this of wives until very
recently. Another reason for choosing this form might be that
the language about the plighting of troths evokes a sense of

hallowed history in what is, after all, a traditional occasion. Fine, but it is to be hoped that couples, clergy and congregations alike will see through the fog of heritage surrounding these fine words to the inequality and unhappiness surrounding them, and avoid them. I hope that when *Common Worship* is revised they will be dropped, even as an option.

The giving and blessing of the rings

The giving and receiving of the rings, and the blessing of these by the priest represents a big development from the Prayer Book marriage service, where provision was made for the giving and receiving of one ring only (no prizes for correctly guessing which partner does what). Neither was there room in the older service for the blessing of the ring. This seemed at the time too much like the veneration or even worship of a mere object and was caught up in the Catholic–Protestant arguments of the sixteenth and seventeenth centuries.

Once again, you have several options. The first is whether you will exchange one or two rings. Whereas there was no provision for the joint giving and receiving of rings in the old service (even though it might still have been done), in the new service the assumption is made that each of you will publicly give a ring to the other. However, provision is made for the giving of only one ring. I hope you agree that the new service is an improvement, and that one ring does not adequately symbolize what is going on. Rather it belongs to a set of assumptions that are no longer relevant: that the man is the provider, and that the wedding, by means of the ring, establishes him as taking the leading role.

Before the rings are exchanged the priest will say one of two short and beautiful prayers. The one in the main text is

Heavenly Father, by your blessing
let *these rings* be to N and N
a symbol of unending love and faithfulness,
to remind them of the vow and covenant
which they have made this day
through Jesus Christ our Lord.

The alternative prayer is

> Heavenly Father, source of everlasting love,
> revealed to us in Jesus Christ
>   and poured into our hearts through your Holy Spirit;
> that love which many waters cannot quench,
>   neither the floods drown;
> that love which is patient and kind, enduring all things
> without end;
> by your blessing, let these rings be to N and N
> symbols to remind them of the covenant made this day
> through your grace in the love of your Son
> and in the power of your Spirit.

In neither prayer are the rings blessed directly, so there is no implication that they become a sort of sacred talisman with special powers to accomplish special ends. What is prayed for is God's blessing on the couple, so that in the marriage the rings convey a special meaning. Both prayers boldly utilize the idea of the covenant which the couple have just made and God and the congregation have just witnessed. Since the surface of a ring has neither beginning nor end, it is an ancient symbol of eternity, highly appropriate to accompany the vows just made to cherish one another until death 'does you part'. I wouldn't want to choose between these prayers. The second one uses words from the Song of Solomon that we have already looked at in this chapter. It also uses a verse of St Paul's eulogy about love, so there can be a link here with two of the readings earlier in the service.

In the old Prayer Book the man says to the woman:

> With this Ring I thee wed, with my body I thee worship,
> and with all my worldly goods I thee endow: in the Name
> of the Father, and of the Son, and of the Holy Ghost.
> Amen.

The joint actions of placing the ring on her finger and saying these words are also 'performative'. Like the vows they are taken to accomplish the 'wed-ding'. The words 'with my body I thee worship' are profound. Only *God* is to be worshipped in Christianity (and in Judaism and Islam). That the bride is to be worshipped in any sense at all is an immensely risky statement, justified by the attitudes of exclusion and devotion and honour that ordinarily speaking belong only to the human response to God. What a pity, therefore, that there was no formal place in the service for the bride to wed the groom, and that according to the laws of the time, she, and all her wealth became his as soon as they became married. In the new order provision is made for the bride and the groom both to exchange words whether or not one ring or two is used. When a ring is given, the words accompanying the gift are

N, I give you this ring
as a sign of our marriage.
With my body I honour you,
all that I am I give to you,
and all that I have I share with you,
within the love of God,
Father, Son and Holy Spirit.

If there is only one ring, the bride says the same words but with one change: '*N*, I *receive* this ring ... ' I wonder whether 'honour' diminishes the more startling 'worship'. What do you think about this? Any losses of emphasis here are gained (aren't they?) by the two lines 'all that I am', and 'all that I have'. You can't get more comprehensive than that! And isn't that little touch 'within the love of God' significant? It adds to the loving atmosphere of the service, and is a reminder that the human love celebrated in the marriage is suffused with the divine love that God is.

The proclamation and blessing of the marriage

In the next section of the service the minister proclaims that you are now husband and wife. Part of what s/he will say at this point is 'I therefore proclaim that they are husband and wife.' The minister has not married you (we will make much of this point in the next chapter). You have married each other by exchanging consent through making your vows, and by the accompanying actions of joining hands and giving and receiving of rings. The minister has not 'performed' anything. You have done it all! Because of what you have both done together, his or her task is to proclaim that you are now married. Part of the kit that ministers may wear is a stole – a sort of decorated scarf. While your hands are joined the priest may wrap the stole around them and tie a knot with it. This is what the popular phrase 'tying the knot' means, and this is where it comes from. The priest will also say, in words which slightly revise an old translation of the saying of Jesus (in Mark 10:9) 'Those whom God has joined together let no one put asunder.' (We will examine the meaning of these words in the last chapter.)

The next task for the priest is to bless you, or more precisely the priest asks God as supreme witness to bless the marriage that has just been solemnized. This is a practice which is emphasized in the churches of the East, where the priest's blessing of the couple (and not the exchange of consent) makes the marriage. In addition to the blessing in the *Common Worship* text, there are five alternative forms or variations (all in the supplementary texts). It is important to look carefully at all of these and choose the one that works best for you both. The blessing is a wonderful prayer, full of joyful, positive words, and pictures of feasting and togetherness. Whichever one you choose will capture the mood of the congregation. They have just seen and heard you marry one another, and every one of them will want to wish you well from the depths of their hearts. They don't need to find their own language for this well-wishing since this beautiful prayer, or any of the alternatives, will do the job:

> Blessed are you, O Lord our God,
> for you have created joy and gladness,
> pleasure and delight, love, peace and fellowship.
> Pour out the abundance of your blessing
> upon N and N in their new life together.
> Let their love for each other be a seal upon their hearts
> and a crown upon their heads.
> Bless them in their work and in their companionship;
> awake and asleep,

in joy and in sorrow,
in life and in death.
Finally, in your mercy, bring them to that banquet
where your saints feast for ever in your heavenly home.
We ask this through Jesus Christ your Son, our Lord,
who lives and reigns with you and the Holy Spirit,
one God, now and for ever.

The blessing will impact on different people in different ways. Reference to the crown is another touch from the East, where it stands for the triumph of love over its foes. You may be struck by how God is thanked and acknowledged as the source of all human joy and gladness; or how the prayer is unabashed in celebrating 'pleasure and delight'; or how the 'pouring out' of the blessing suggests a good wine; or how the reference to feasting links the reception to the biblical picture of the end of time; or, or, or . . . Let the words flow through you and around you.

The registration

The signing of the registers is scheduled to happen next. Again there is a choice: do you want to have the registers signed here, during the service (the new position), or afterwards (the old position)? There are at least three obvious advantages to having the signing now. The first is the integrity of the ceremony itself. The wedding is not legally recognized until the registers are signed, and the bringing of the legal and social recognition of the marriage right into the ceremony heightens its importance. It also provides an opportunity for an extra hymn, or for recorded music, or for any of your musical friends to play or sing a suitable song or piece of music. And if the signing takes place here the service can end on a high note, immediately after the prayers. You must both sign the registers, with a minimum of two witnesses, usually one of the bride's and one of the groom's parents and the priest.

The prayers

The prayers which are offered for you both at the end of the service are, in a word, magnificent. Sensitive, loving, reverent and heart-felt, they are offered by the priest and congregation to God for the full flourishing of your marriage. The prayers follow four themes, and it would be usual to have at least one prayer within each theme. The themes are 'Thanksgiving' (to God for you both and for your marriage), prayers for your 'Spiritual growth', prayers for the gifts of 'Faithfulness, joy, love, forgiveness and healing' and prayers for 'Children, other family members and friends'. Finally the Lord's Prayer is said (in the traditional or more modern version). However, there is a big surprise. In the on-line version of the service, if you go to the section 'Prayers' and click on 'here', you will find an extra 27 'additional prayers' that can be used at this point in the service. They are all grouped around the four themes, and they are all numbered for ease of selection. It would be hard to find prayers more sensitive, relevant and inclusive than these. An evening downloading them, reading them, comparing them and then choosing from them would be an evening of pure discovery and delight. And, of course, you can ask your minister to use some of these prayers even if you are not using this service or being married in an Anglican church.

It is impossible to discuss the choice of prayers in any detail, but I cannot resist the opportunity, late in the chapter, to suggest at least the flavour of these prayers. Do you like the sound of

Let peace spring from their faithfulness to each other
and flow deeper with the passing years?

Or,

Let goodness flower with forgiveness
and be the fruit of their married life?

Or,

In gentleness let them be tender with each other's dreams
and healing of each other's wounds?

These sentiments (they are called 'petitions') are all found in the first additional prayer. There is also a prayer for absent friends:

> May friends and family gathered here,
> and those separated by distance,
> be strengthened and blessed this day.

There is a prayer for everyone who has witnessed your vows:

> Grant that all those who have witnessed these vows
> may find their lives strengthened
> and their loyalties confirmed,

as well as several prayers for the sharing of love, and one for your home:

> Lord and Saviour Jesus Christ,
> who shared at Nazareth the life of an earthly home:
> reign in the home of these your servants as Lord and
> King ...

There is a prayer (no. 14) that even thanks God for 'your gift of sexual love' and asks that you both 'remain lovers' all your days. There is a prayer 'for the healing of memory' especially apt if the marriage has been preceded by pain of any kind. There is a prayer that you will 'reach old age in the company of friends'. There are prayers for each of your families (no. 26), for the support of your friends (no. 27) and a particularly moving prayer (no. 25) 'for an existing family', which may do much to create new ties of friendship in particular circumstances:

> God of all grace and goodness,
> we thank you for this new family,
> and for everything parents and children have to share;
> by your Spirit of peace draw them together
> and help them to be true friends to one another ...

Don't forget, if you want to write your own prayers, or your parents or friends want to write prayers, the minister will usually be keen to encourage and assist. S/he may want to see them first, just to advise about their appropriateness. After the prayers there remains the last hymn, the 'dismissal' said by the priest, and your grand exit down the aisle to your chosen music.

We have worked through the Marriage Service in this chapter. I hope you agree that it is a wonderful treasury of words, freely available to you, with fine opportunities for you to work through and select the material that appeals to you. With all this available, is there anyone who will knowingly settle for less?

Notes

1. www.statistics.gov.uk/registration/Marriage. Accessed 19 November 2002.
2. This is one of two 'Prayers at the Calling of the Banns' from the supplementary texts of the *Common Worship* marriage service, available at www.cofe.anglican.org Accessed 22 November 2002.
3. Section 4.3.
4. See the Anglican Faculty Office, web address above, or phone them on 020 7222 5381.
5. Lake, S. (2000), *Using Common Worship Marriage: A Practical Guide to the New Services*. London: Church House Publishing.
6. In all these quotations the italics are mine.
7. *Celebration Hymnal, Vol. 2* (music edn). (There are no page numbers, only hymn numbers, in this hymn book.)
8. The body responsible for overseeing the copyright of hymns and worship songs is Christian Copyright Licensing International. Contact them and use their 'song search' facility at www.ccli.co.uk. Accessed 22 November 2002.
9. Accessed 22 November 2002.
10. Accessed 22 November 2002.
11. See Lake, *Using Common Worship Marriage*, p. 43.
12. It has been pointed out to me that 'I will' is the present tense of the verb 'to will', and because this is the verb used here, the meaning is in the present tense. I think the tense is future. It is an answer to the future tense question 'Will you take . . . ?', and it is short for 'Yes, I will take . . . ' For the

arguments, see Thatcher, *Marriage after Modernity*, pp. 110–14, and *Living Together*, pp. 189–201.

13. See Stuart, E. (1995), *Just Good Friends: Towards a Lesbian and Gay Theology of Relationships*. London: Mowbrays, p. 131 and the references there.

14. This is well explained by Lake, *Using Common Worship Marriage*, p. 48.

6

The Spirit of Our Marriage

The main theme of the book has been how a church wedding can enrich your marriage. I hope that that case has by now been well and truly proved. The present chapter follows the path of an earlier argument: that the wedding is the most significant point in the journey into the adventure of Christian marriage; that it presupposes a shared personal history leading to the wedding, and a further history extending beyond it. The problem is that no one preparing for the wedding is really preparing for the experience of the marriage that follows it. There is the anxiety and drama of the big event, the rush away from it (preferably to an exotic location, misnamed the 'honeymoon') and then an escalation of normality. This chapter sets out to perform two tasks. First it will suggest that *the religious resources on which you have drawn for your church marriage can help sustain your marriage and your happiness within it.* Second it will suggest that many people who have a church wedding have one not because they think of themselves as religious but because they think of themselves as *spiritual* people. This takes us into exciting territory, the new venture of marital spirituality. So first we will look at some of the further landmarks along the marital way; then we will take some tentative steps into 'the spirit of marriage'. The prize within our grasp here is worth waiting for. A richer understanding of marriage can enrich the marriage itself.

After the wedding

Your wedding is already likely to have been located relatively late in your personal life journeys. The 'long path to the nuptials' may already have led you away from the home of your upbringing to independent living, and perhaps to sharing the marital home prior to the wedding. Since the gap between leaving school and becoming married has lengthened considerably in a single generation, the transition from the parental home to the marital home is increasingly indirect, perhaps involving halls of residence, sharing a flat, renting a room, or other temporary accommodation. The transition is less abrupt than it would have been had you married ten years or so earlier. Nonetheless, as many writers point out, we may still bring lots of baggage from the parental home that is best left at the door of the new home and not allowed in! Indeed one psychotherapist disconcertingly suggests that when we first make love with our partners there are six people in the bed![1] Perhaps the transition from the family home to the marital home is harder to accomplish emotionally than one or both of you thought it would be? Or again, perhaps one or more of the parents will not let go, and you are slow to catch on to your partner's exasperation about this? The point is that the bonding between newly married partners can be threatened by the baggage and continuing presence of the parental home in the new home. 'Unless, however, an individual marrying has sufficiently left to establish clear and flexible boundaries in relation to family of origin, that bonding may come eventually to feel like suffocation or invasion.'[2] Understanding the difficulty is the main means of dealing satisfactorily with it.

Or again, if the first marital home is a 'starter-home' it may be less than the ideal home you want for your marriage. It might be too cramped, too dark, too old, too cold, too noisy and too close to the neighbours for you to make the noises you want or need to. Whatever your preferences for type of home you will need the physical space to develop both the separateness and the togetherness needed for a balanced marriage. This need is not immediately obvious, but can easily be a source of creeping irritation or conflict. Or again, later marriages create new urgency about the decision whether to have children. There is a whole clutch of issues that arise here. You are both likely to be working full-time. Children will require an interruption to their mother's career, and mothers feel differently about this. Some wives will welcome motherhood as itself a fulfilling and wonderfully worthwhile time of their lives, with less paid work and much-reduced career prospects a small price to pay. Others will want to combine motherhood and career. Either way agreement between husband and wife about these matters is essential, and unless they are talked about agreement will be unlikely. The gentle support of the husband at a time of his wife's reduced economic independence and withdrawal from the labour market may be vital at this time.

Or again, you may be thinking of moving to a bigger home with space for a nursery, but that will require a bigger mortgage at the same time as a reduction in your joint income is looming. That in turn may lead to further postponement of the decision about children. And then there may a lack of clarity about what the decision is. Is it 'Yes, now', 'Yes, but later', 'No, not now', or 'No, never'? Well Even 'Yes, now' may lead to some anxiety if conception does not result, and indeed it may not, since 10 per cent of all couples have infertility problems which require medical consultation. (Infertility is usually defined as a disease or condition of the reproductive system diagnosed after a couple has had one year of unprotected, well-timed intercourse, or the inability to carry a pregnancy to term.) 'Yes, but later' requires indefinite postponement when time is no longer on your side, and 'No, not now' may mean different things, like 'Let's review it soon', or 'Let's keep our options open', and this may conceal different expectations or desires. Or again, let's suppose you are among the growing number of married couples who prefer not to have children. One of you may change your mind, the other not. And you may conceive anyway. At the very least, there may be a range of unforeseen problems that arise about extending the family.

Or again, these problems may be as nothing when compared with the real arrival of a real baby. I remember intense joy at the birth of our son coupled with relief about his and his mother's excellent health, after previous disappointments. Even the deepest joy will not be unaffected by the frightening responsibility for that mysterious bundle of demanding and vulnerable personhood. But the marriage can be vulnerable too at this stage. There will be great disruption to established routines, the continuing upheaval of your social life, interrupted nights and the problem of tiredness and the cumulative shock at all the accommodations being made to the new household member, not to mention the possible shades of husband's jealousy as a new and permanent rival to his wife's time, attention and body arrives together with his or her list of non-negotiable demands.

So far we have done no more than mention some of the possible causes of disruption to the equilibrium of your marriage. Other possible causes, like arguments over money (or power), or later possible causes of disruption, like mid-life crises, children leaving and the onset of ageing, have been omitted. Marriage preparation, as we have seen, is supposed to anticipate some of the tensions that are going to arise in any marriage and to begin to equip couples to deal with them. The purpose of this chapter is not to elaborate the difficulties but to make suggestions about the contribution that religious faith, or a sense of spirituality, however tenuous, might itself contribute to resolving these tensions. Talk of spirituality or of spiritual growth can be a real turn-off. It may suggest private religious practices that have long been abandoned, or it may (wrongly) assume that in order to talk about spirituality at all we must first split the spirit off from the body, leaving us, of course, with what the philosopher Gilbert Ryle, and following him the pop singer Sting, called 'the ghost in the machine'.[3] A second misconception about spirituality is that achievements in this area, such as becoming a more spiritual person, are always accomplished alone as a solitary person, perhaps communing alone with God in a monastic cell or a very private room. But both these misconceptions have to be discarded. Suppose spiritual growth is about becoming a more loving, balanced, sensitive person: doesn't that make spiritual growth worthwhile? And suppose (rightly) that this process of becoming cannot be accomplished privately, silently, or even religiously, but only in cooperation with close 'others': doesn't that make marriage a fine opportunity, 'place', laboratory even, both for one's own spiritual growth and for that of one's spouse?

The fact that you are having a church wedding already suggests you are likely to answer 'yes' to these questions. So, before we talk any more about that vague word 'spirituality' it is necessary to make its meanings a bit more precise. There are literally hundreds of definitions of spirituality, so I'm going to concentrate on just two: one Christian, the other humanist. Jesus said,

> 'Love the Lord your God with all your heart, with all your soul, and with all your mind.' That is the greatest, the first commandment. The second is like it: 'Love your neighbour as yourself.' Everything in the law and the prophets hangs on these two commandments. (Matthew 22:37–40)

Since the love of God and neighbour is fundamental to the practice of faith, I think it fair to say spiritual people are those who try to love God (however that is expressed) and to love their neighbours as themselves. That will have to do as the Christian definition (and people of other faiths may have little difficulty with it). The humanist definition is a shorter version, leaving out God. Spiritual people love their neighbours as themselves. Of course there is more that can be added, but this is a start. Being a spiritual person is being a loving person. Religious and non-religious people might at least agree on that. And when our 'neighbour' is our spouse, the response of neighbour-love will be at its most testing and intense.

Circles of love

Mutual ministries

There is a huge and exciting idea generated by the doctrine that marriage is a sacrament. As we saw in Chapter 2 there is disagreement between Christians about whether marriage should be included in the list of the church's sacraments. That is probably why *Common Worship* avoids the term. Equally there is agreement among Christians that marriage, whether or not described as a sacrament, provides a special channel for God's grace to flow into the world. These preliminaries can divert us from the important point that in traditional Western thought the sacrament of marriage is the only sacrament not administered by the minister. S/he cannot marry you or cause the grace of God to flow into your marriage. You marry each other.[4] That in turn raises the question about who the minister of the sacrament actually is. The answer is simple and unambiguous: you are both the ministers of the sacrament that is your marriage. You may not see yourself or fancy yourself as a minister of anything *at all*. Too bad. In the marriage service each partner is minister to the other of the sacrament of marriage. The questions remain how this forgotten detail may be significant today.

I want to make two points about this. First, if you are joint ministers of the sacrament which is your marriage, you are co-equal partners in the marriage. Joint ministry is a fine basis for equal regard and full mutuality over every detail of the marriage. You are full and equal partners in that common enterprise. No room for obedience here! Second, everything you do for each other is a ministry, or an 'ad*minister*ing' of the sacrament. One of the supplementary prayers in the marriage service comes near to saying this when the priest asks God to

> Give them wisdom and devotion in ordering their common life,
> that each may be to the other
> a strength in need, a counsellor in perplexity,
> a comfort in sorrow and a companion in joy.

In another *Common Worship* service there is a prayer, which runs:

> Give grace to us, our families and friends, and to all our neighbours,
> that we may serve Christ in one another, and love as he loves us.[5]

There is a profound insight in this prayer that is particularly applicable to marriage. When we 'serve' each other, it is as if we also serve Christ himself.

When I wrote about the joint ministry of the sacrament of marriage in *Marriage after Modernity* I had to think of examples of little ways by which, in fact, married partners do accomplish this ministry to each other. My list included:

earning money, doing chores, choosing and enjoying holidays, celebrating birthdays, shopping, balancing responsibilities of home and work, caring for one another while sick, making up quickly after rows, making love, making meals and washing up after them, making separate spaces as well as forging joint activities, and enlarging ... mutual love in order to embody it more widely in church and community ... [6]

While language about sacrament, and sacramental ministry will not appeal to everyone, what is being said under the surface is important for everyone because it is about what love requires in the particular 'estate' of marriage. So we become 'spiritual', or exercise 'marital spirituality' in the most simple and common ways.

Deepening love

The marriage service contains several prayers that your love for one another will deepen. Marriage is given, we recall, as 'the foundation of family life' in which 'each member of the family, in good times and in bad, may find strength, companionship and comfort, and *grow to maturity in love*'. In another prayer the congregation prays for you in these words:

> Gracious God,
> accept our prayers for N and N,
> that *as their love ripens*
> *and their marriage matures*
> they may reap the harvest of the Spirit,
> rejoice in your gifts
> and reflect your glory in Christ Jesus our Lord.

God is asked in another prayer to 'Sow in their lives the joy that comes from sharing and grows with giving.' And indeed, the very vows

> to have and to hold
> from this day forward;

for better, for worse,
for richer, for poorer,
in sickness and in health,
to love and to cherish,
till death us do part

suggest that love grows as it faces and overcomes adversity. Adversity, then, can itself be a stimulus to renewed commitment and deepening love. Now there may be nothing untoward about these prayers. However, if love were to 'ripen' and marriages were to 'mature' automatically, then there would be no need to pray for it to happen. The thinking behind these prayers is that love does not automatically ripen and marriages do not automatically mature, but with God's help it could be more likely. But how, exactly?

A recent study of perceptions of love may help with the answer. Love for a partner, it was found, may often comprise three elements.[7] The first is *intimacy*; the second is *passion* (defined as 'a state of intense longing for union with another');[8] and the third is *commitment*, understood both as the decision to love another person and to maintain that love. 'Romantic love' is a combination of intimacy and passion, but without commitment. 'Companionate love' is a 'blend of the intimacy and decision/commitment components of love', typically found in marriages in which the physical attraction has 'died down'; while 'consummate love' is the abiding combination of intimacy, passion and commitment in a long-term relationship. The author concludes: 'A warm, companionable, central relationship is, for most people, a crucial ingredient of a happy and fulfilling life – but love alone will not sustain it.'[9]

The love that 'will not sustain' a marriage is the one that has not moved beyond the earlier phases of love. Given that descriptions of love will inevitably be imprecise, and the types of love will overlap, it may nonetheless be possible to trace the evolution of deepening love through the various phases that might be called intimate love, passionate love, romantic love, companionate love and consummate love. Intimacy and passion belong together. Passion need never die (even though it often does), but it needs to be supplemented by other kinds of love, which may become increasingly important. Romantic love may combine intimacy and passion with elements of companionship. Popular culture is saturated with overvalued romantic love and the aftermaths of its demise. We could say that at this level love is maintained but only because mutual satisfactions are gained by it. That means we may be interested in a loving relationship primarily for what we may get out of it. When tiredness or boredom breaks in and there are no long-term commitments, copping-out happens – often with much pain to the other partner. With love at this level only, there may be reason to stay together 'for richer' and 'in health', but no reason to stay together 'for poorer' and 'in sickness'. When companionate love becomes consummate love, passion and mutual satisfaction are not extinguished but transcended in the commitments that couples make to each other. The love which loves the other for the other's sake, and not merely for 'my' sake, is the love that God is. A marriage consciously founded on this is one that is likely to be happy and lasting, whether or not the partners hold explicit religious beliefs. That is one way whereby God's grace can enrich a marriage. Through the practice of deep neighbour-love that marriage requires, God's own love is realized. Consummate love, then, requires spirituality to achieve it. Even if you do not believe in God or name God 'Love', you may assent, and assent quite strongly, to most of the analysis of the different loves attempted here.

Anderson and Fite speak of 'the loss of illusions that must take place'[10] if marital love is to deepen. In the passionate phase of love, the desire for the other can override a more sober estimate of one's partner's foibles or habits. Less clouded perceptions of our partner's shortcomings should have dawned upon us long before the wedding, but they will continue to arrive afterwards, when deepening commitment may take care of them. More important, the talking-up of marriage can create illusory expectations of bliss, which, if set too high, will inevitably produce disappointment or even resentment, if the letdown into ordinariness is painfully bumpy. (I wondered whether to include the section on marriage as a sacrament for just this reason. It kept its place because God's grace comes through the sheer ordinariness of much of our existence.)

The prayers in the service also include references to your ability to learn from your failures, to make a loving home, to hospitality in the home, to your contribution to your village or street, to your relations with families and friends, and to any children you may have. These are some of the contexts where committed love is given an opportunity to deepen. So, for example, the prayer

Give them patience with their failures
and persistence with their hopes

may acquire a new resonance after a series of rows and disappointments. A prayer, worth a recall when you are rushing round making a meal or preparing the spare room for yet more guests, is

May the hospitality of their home
bring refreshment and joy to all around them;
may their love overflow to neighbours in need
and embrace those in distress.

The optional prayer,

Bestow on them, if it is your will,
the heritage and gift of children
and the grace to bring them up
to know you, to love you and to serve you

does not commit you to having children, but prepares you for the possibility and the great responsibility they lay upon you. There is even a prayer (to be used when a divorced or bereaved person marries again), 'for an existing family', which runs

God of all grace and goodness,
we thank you for this new family,
and for everything parents and children have to share;
by your Spirit of peace draw them together
and help them to be true friends to one another.
Let your love surround them

and your care protect them;
through Jesus Christ our Lord.

These and other matters are found in the marriage service partly because it is by living through them, and the demanding changes that accompany them, that God's grace is really needed and given in the form of deepening love.

Balancing 'covenant' and 'union'

A deadly assumption within a marriage is that once we marry we are no longer separate individuals, but, so to speak, a newly forged corporate identity of two, in which each of us gets lost, especially the partner with the lesser self-esteem. This is a situation that can be positively overcome by utilizing the 'models' of marriage encountered in Chapter 2. Applying the symbols of covenant and union to marriage simultaneously, and counter-balancing each with the other can find the solution to the problem of separateness within togetherness, and togetherness within separateness. The notion of 'covenant' clearly empha-sizes your separate identities as wife and husband as you undertake a common project, whereas the one-flesh union clearly emphasizes your oneness, the 'union of hearts and lives'. I think it is helpful for spouses to see themselves as simul-taneously separate persons and united partners. The two defin-ing poles of a marriage are not 'husband' and 'wife', but rather more subtlely, separateness and togetherness, for each of you remains separate as a person, yet each of you is together in the unity of marriage. Sometimes these opposites of concepts are called 'polarities' (pole-arities), and a rule about polarities is that one can't function unless the other does. Fifty years ago a famous Christian teacher warned against couples regarding their union as an 'amalgamation in which the identity of the con-stituents is swallowed up and lost in an undifferentiated unity'.[11] This used to be a particular danger for wives, who may have been expected to assume their husband's identity, just as they are still expected to assume his name. The opposite danger is that a marriage becomes 'a mere conjunction in which no real union is involved'. In such extreme cases, the couple's separateness prevents their union from being established. Anderson and Fite go so far as to say becoming married '*means* learning how to live with being separate and becoming connected at the same time'. They describe in a variety of ways how this may happen:

> ... one must leave in order to cleave; having a home with a room of one's own; keeping separate and keeping connected; bonding and differentiating. The wedding, which occurs in the midst of parallel processes of leaving and cleaving, is the occasion for shifting the emphasis from differentiating to bonding without overlooking each unique person.[12]

Another writer has spoken of the three identities which spouses possess, namely those of spouses, parents and individuals.[13] A marriage is more likely to flourish when each of these three roles is attended to and nurtured. A husband and a wife are simultaneously a person, a partner, and (probably at some time) a parent. Attending to one another's needs in all three roles might constitute the first basic task of marital spirituality.

Second, we can say that a couple whose partners are *inter*dependent is more balanced than one where the partners are either independent from, or dependent upon, each other. Independence turns separation into isolation: dependence turns union into a burdensome loss of identity. Couples will want to distinguish for themselves between oppressive and non-oppressive elements which together comprise their union. A marital union which creates dependence or assumes a fusion of individuals into a single synthesis is a distortion of marriage. Conversely, a union which exists through mutual presence, intimate communication and reciprocal love of the separate persons is a balanced whole, what was called in the medieval church, a partnership (*consortium*) of the whole of life (*omnis vitae*). Pope John Paul II said 'The communion between God and his people finds its definitive fulfilment in Jesus Christ, the bridegroom who loves and gives himself as the savior of humanity, uniting it to himself as his body.'[14] What this means is that Christians compare two types of relationship for similarities and differences: the one the relationship between God and humankind, the other the relationship between spouses. The central truth of Christianity is that God became embodied in humankind as Jesus Christ. Jesus is the union of God with humankind, yet Jesus is also a human self like ourselves, and so is both united with God and separate from God at the same time. In a similar way spouses are united into a single marriage, while remaining distinct selves. The experience of being married might actually help people to understand what is sometimes called 'the mystery of the Incarnation', because that experience precisely involves being separate and being united at the same time.

André Guindon, another Roman Catholic, was commendably wary of the 'one-flesh' angle on Christian marriage if the opposite pole of separation unbalanced it. He thought any marital arrangement whereby a spouse abandoned his or her freedom or was required to surrender it would compromise the spouse as a person. 'Nothing of worth would be left for the other to love. The very basis for human otherness would be lacking.' Why? Because 'any dissolution of oneself into a kind of two-in-one being would amount to a moral suicide'. What was needed, he thought, was 'an interchange of intimate communication between the spouses which gradually makes them uniquely present to each other – to each other's bodies, minds, needs, feelings, hearts, desires, fears, hurts, joys, and dreams'.[15] Another profound writer on the spirituality of marriage uses the thoughtful illustration of two interacting circles to explain the interaction of married partners. In the ideal marriage (which does not, of course, exist!) as each partner grows closer to the other, each becomes 'more permeable' to the other, while 'neither absorbing nor being absorbed' by the other. Using the familiar geometrical figure of the overlapping circles, she says:

> The circles actually begin to overlap, creating a spiritual reality which is both 'I' and 'not I', 'Thou' and 'not Thou', significantly and recognizably both two and one. When a pair goes from closeness to commitment, each comes to be partly other as well as self. It is no longer spiritually accurate to consider one alone, in isolation from the conjugal dimension that pervades it.[16]

Perhaps the image of the overlapping 'circles of love' is the best one we have to explain separateness and togetherness?

The 'ethos' of the marriage

In a marriage which rests in Christian understanding, each partner tries to love the other as God loves them both. And each partner (as we saw in the prayers earlier in the chapter) tries to recognize Christ in the other. While this suggestion may sound pie-in-the-sky to ears unattuned to religious language, it does in fact make good sense. In the Christian faith, Christ is divine, and as such is to be worshipped, indeed adored. Christ, as the subject and the object of faith, is therefore to be taken with unconditional seriousness. We may recall how the old Prayer Book marriage service encourages us to 'worship' our partners. Recognizing Christ in the other, then, is no elusive search for a ghostly religious image, but the acknowledgment that our devotion to our beloved is fundamentally a sacred attitude, a holy way of life. I call this the 'ethos' of Christian marriage.[17] Anderson and Fite call it the 'marital habitus' or what it means 'to take the covenant partner in abiding seriousness'.[18] Their analysis coincides largely with mine, but they give priority to sacrifice, justice and reconciliation. All of these are core values for Christians, and all have an important place in marriage.

Their definition of sacrifice is 'the willingness to forgo the benefits of particular choices for the sake of another's well-being because we hold that person in abiding seriousness'.[19] If power is not shared in the marriage, sacrifice can quickly become demeaning. If the partners hold an equal regard for each other, sacrifice is sometimes necessary: without equal regard it reduces esteem and can destroy a marriage. As Anderson and Fite say:

> When one partner does all the accommodating or when the sacrifices are unevenly distributed over time, the covenant of mutuality is distorted and the marriage is not just. The marriage may be stable. It may even be a happy relationship. But it is not just. The insistence that opportunities for growth and self-determination are available to women as well as men is an illustration of justice in

marriage. A balanced distribution of power and the maintenance of equal regard are both necessary if we are to establish covenantal relationships that are just. Marriages that endure are able to keep alive the paradox of self-determination and sacrifice.[20]

There will be countless times within a marriage when upsets will require reconciliation one way or another. This too is a major theme of the Christian story, which insists that God has reconciled everyone to God's own self. Reconciliation then, is certain to be a virtue within Christian marriage, but this is not to say that forgiveness can be demanded or that the practice of reconciliation can allow the cause of estrangement to remain unrectified. Once again, Anderson and Fite get this right. They say:

> The possibility of reconciliation in marriage is determined not so much by the severity of the break as by the depth of the will to reconcile and be reconciled. The practice of reconciliation in a marriage is an extension of the *readiness to take the covenantal partner in abiding seriousness*. Taking another person seriously means acknowledging the violation and experiencing the pain of a promise broken.[21]

Another writer uses the contrast between two types of movement to show how exciting the development of marital spirituality can be. The two types are 'centrifugal' and 'centripetal'. A centrifugal force is one that tends to impel a thing or part of a thing outward from a centre of rotation. A centripetal force is one that keeps an object moving in a circular path and is directed inward toward the centre of rotation. Traditional spirituality emphasizes centrifugal movement, away from the self as the centre of the world. Marital spirituality emphasizes centripetal movement, 'revolving around the axis created by its own being, the axis defining two as standing in relation'. That is why 'the primary spiritual task of conjugal love is the creation, maintenance, and growth of that unique reality which is, in each new relation, the necessary foundation for joint outward-looking service'.[22]

The hope is maintained that a 'loving relationship of itself produces antibodies against egotism and provides a training ground for creating wider and wider circles of love'.[23] This writer is very conscious of the havoc that exploitative relationships can cause. Even so, she affirms that 'attraction, desire and longing are spiritually worth the risk, for they force us continually outward to learn the lessons of unity'. Love and longing are good for us, for 'they break down our ego boundaries, allowing the self to be enlarged and enriched by knowing others, by learning from them and interacting with them'.[24] The psychological content of her writing is rooted in Christian conviction. Married love, she says, is itself a 'spiritual discipline' because it 'can pleasurably tempt one toward self-forgetfulness and self-transcendence'. What moves us in the other may be nothing less than a revelation of God: 'The recognition of "God" in another, our attraction to this revelation, and the affinity it brings into being are the basis for spiritual friendship as well as for the more intimate conjugal relations.'

So when married people practise spirituality or spiritual growth, they can make no progress at all without one another. It is a shared enterprise like the marriage itself. Marital spirituality is the practise of mutual love which expands even as it negotiates difficulties. For many people, this mutual love has a religious basis, which may provide a greater depth in understanding and resource in crisis.

Notes

1. In a workshop at the Smart Marriages Conference, Orlando, FL (June 2001).
2. Anderson, H. and Fite, R. C. (1993), *Becoming Married*. Louisville, KY: Westminster/John Knox Press, p. 74.
3. Ryle, G. (1963), *The Concept of Mind*. Harmondsworth: Peregrine Books, p. 17; Sting, 'Ghost in the Machine'.
4. For a fuller explanation, see Thatcher, *Marriage after Modernity*, pp. 213–17.
5. www.cofe.anglican.org Accessed 2 December 2002.
6. Thatcher, *Marriage after Modernity* p. 241.

7. Sternberg, R. J. (1988), 'Triangulating love', in R. J. Sternberg and M. L. Barnes (eds), *The Psychology of Love*. New Haven, CT: Yale University Press, cit., M. Tysoe (1992), *Love Isn't Quite Enough: The Psychology of Male–Female Relationships*. London: HarperCollins/Fontana, pp. 20–25.
8. Hatfield, E. (1988), 'Passionate and companionate love', in Sternberg and Barnes, *The Psychology of Love*, p. 193.
9. Tysoe, *Love Isn't Quite Enough*, p. 202.
10. Anderson and Fite, *Becoming Married*, p. 113.
11. Bailey, D. S. (1952), *The Mystery of Love and Marriage*. London: Camelot Press, p. 44.
12. Anderson and Fite, *Becoming Married*, p. 115 (emphasis added).
13. Hogan, M. M. (1993), *Finality and Marriage*. Marquette Studies in Philosophy: Marquette, MI: Marquette University Press, p. 102.
14. John Paul II (1981), *Familiaris Consortio*. Vatican City: Vatican Press, section 13. Online version at www.cin.org/jp2ency/famcon.html. Accessed 3 December 2002.
15. Guindon, A. (1986), *The Sexual Creators: An Ethical Proposal for Concerned Christians*. Lanham, MD: University Press of America, p. 97.
16. Oliver, M. A. M. (1994), *Conjugal Spirituality: The Primacy of Mutual Love in Christian Tradition*. Kansas City, KS: Sheed & Ward, p. 45 (author's emphasis).
17. Thatcher, *Marriage after Modernity*, p. 215.
18. Anderson and Fite, *Becoming Married*, p. 151.
19. Anderson and Fite, *Becoming Married*, p. 152.
20. Anderson and Fite, *Becoming Married*, p. 153.
21. Anderson and Fite, *Becoming Married*, p. 155.
22. Oliver, *Conjugal Spirituality*, p. 53.
23. Oliver, *Conjugal Spirituality*, p. 105.
24. Oliver, *Conjugal Spirituality*, p. 52.

7

Second Time Around?

Can I marry in church a second time?

If you are thinking about marrying again, and being married in church, you are in a position of great sensitivity and you may be worried in case your private and deeply personal circumstances are not treated with quite the recognition and respect they deserve. If your first husband or wife has died, then you will be dealing with bereavement and private grief. You and your new partner will both need to be assured that you have, as far as is humanly possible, come to terms with the loss of your spouse and (in all probability) with living alone. You will both need to know that you are emotionally ready to make the binding commitment to your new partner that the ceremony will solemnize. If you have been bereaved and approach a priest with a view to marrying again in church, at least you can know in advance that he or she will have no doctrinal or moral problem about conducting your new wedding. S/he may wish to be satisfied that you are ready to take this gigantic personal step, but this will be an expression of pastoral concern for you both rather than any judgement that the doctrine or law of the church prevents or casts doubt on it.

Putting asunder?

Problems arise, as you will already know, when you are divorced and your former partner is alive. In the first part of this chapter we are going to look at the teaching of some of the churches about marrying again, so you can begin to know how a request for a second marriage is likely to be received. In the second half, we will look at some questions you may ask yourselves and questions clergy may ask you if you are about to remarry. The big issue for the churches is that (commendably enough) they all want to witness to the teaching of Jesus about marriage. Our problem is that they do this in quite different ways, and the meaning of the teaching of Jesus is open to different and legitimate interpretations. All the churches hold that marriage is a life-long commitment until death. There are some places in the Christian scriptures where we seem to be told that a person may not marry again when the former partner is still alive. Let's look at two of these now. In the same place where Jesus says, 'It follows that they are no longer two individuals: they are one flesh' (Matthew 19:5–6, Mark 10:9: see Chapter 2 above), he adds, 'Those whom God has joined together, let no one separate' (or 'put asunder').[1] And in his letter to the Romans St Paul wrote:

> You must be aware, my friends – I am sure you have some knowledge of law – that a person is subject to the law only so long as he is alive. For example, a married woman is by law bound to her husband while he lives; but if the husband dies, she is released from the marriage bond. If, therefore, in her husband's lifetime she gives herself to another man, she will be held to be an adulteress; but if her husband dies, she is free of the law and she does not commit adultery by giving herself to another man. (Romans 7:3)

These texts have a long history of interpretation in the West, and the dominant interpretation has been that divorce and remarriage are forbidden. On this view, the church cannot sanction divorce because God does not permit human beings to 'put asunder' those whom God has joined. This view was arrived at quite early in the church's history. While 'separation' was allowed (and this may have been *called* 'divorce'), remarriage was not allowed, because the marriage was regarded as lasting until the death of one of the partners. So when churches have refused to allow remarriage, we can at least be clear why they do so. The motivation is not negative judgement about anyone's suitability for remarriage (although it has often sounded like it), but because of the belief that Jesus Christ himself forbade it. No one can remarry when their former partner is still alive because the church has no authority from God to pronounce the marriage void. People who think this, think marriage is 'indissoluble' (and have been called 'indissolubilists').[2]

Divorce and the churches

So let's review very briefly what the official teaching about remarrying is in the Roman Catholic, Orthodox, Protestant and Anglican parts of the one great church of Christ before return- ing to the meaning of these texts. The Roman Catholic view remains the one just described (although there are exceptions). But this view is not what it seems. While the Roman Catholic Church will not recognize divorce, it does recognize 'that many broken marriages were never in fact true marriages'.[3] Marriages can be 'annulled'. Annulment differs from divorce in assuming that there never was a valid marriage in the first place. Since there never was a marriage, divorce is thereby unnecessary, and indeed impossible.

How does the Roman Catholic Church tell whether an appar- ently valid marriage was not a real marriage after all? One way of doing this is to show that the exchange of consent, the cen- tral point of the marriage liturgy, was 'defective' in some way. But, how defective? A common ground of defective consent is 'lack of due discretion', and further enquiry into this reveals many examples.[4] I choose three, merely to illustrate the breadth of possibilities that exist:

1   The woman of happily married parents who is so infatuated with the man she proposes to marry that she is either blind to his serious faults or assumes he will change them when he is married ...
2   The man who expects to retain control of his earnings, giving an inadequate amount to his wife for the upkeep of the family and home whilst retaining the balance to finance his new cars and frequently changing hobbies ...
3   The woman who lost her father at a young age and marries

a man who is considerably older than her and to whom she does not feel sexually attracted.

It is clear that many psychological and social considerations are relevant to judgements about defective consent. The point, however, is that the Roman Catholic position regarding divorce is unique among the churches (no divorce) and much more liberal than most people (especially non-Catholics) believe. If you need more information about this, a good place to start is to contact Marriage Care at www.marriagecare.org.uk.[5]

The number of Orthodox Christians in Britain is small, but they belong to an equally ancient church tradition (numerous in the East), and they are mentioned here because their view about divorce deserves to be heard, and has much to commend to other Christians and churches. Like the Roman Catholics they believe that marriage is a sacrament and lasts for life (and indeed beyond this life and into the next). They also believe that human sinfulness is all-pervasive, and that some people are not always able, through weakness, to keep their vows. So, while the end of a marriage would be regarded as a serious spiritual disaster, nevertheless it would be recognized as having ended. The ground for this is sometimes called 'spiritual death'. How do the Orthodox regard the words of Jesus, 'Those whom God has joined together, let no one separate'? They think that no human being can separate people that God has joined. But they also think that *God can* separate those people that God has joined. And since God has entrusted to the church full authority over the sacraments, the church in God's name is able to pronounce a marriage spiritually dead. In these circumstances either partner is free to marry again.[6]

The Protestant churches have a freer attitude to divorce and remarriage. Since the Christian scriptures are (arguably) restrictive about divorce and Protestants appeal directly to the Bible in shaping their teachings, this is surprising and requires further explanation. At the Reformation in the sixteenth century, all Protestants held that the Roman Catholic Church was wrong in thinking marriage was a sacrament. In some respects they lowered its status. The appeal to St Paul's teaching that it provided a divinely appointed solution to the problem of sexual desire reactivated a rather base justification for marriage. And (this is where the appeal to the Bible is most apparent) it was noted that the Christian scriptures themselves clearly allowed exceptions to the 'no divorce' rule.[7] The emphasis in Protestantism on personal sin, the need to repent of it, and the possibility of a fresh start in life, assisted by the grace of God (all 'hardcore' gospel values rightly emphasized by evangelical Christians today) has been transferred positively to the understanding of marriage, allowing a fresh start to be made here too.

In one Protestant church (the Methodist Church) more than half of the marriages (62 per cent) conducted in 1996 involved at least one divorced person.[8] In the United Reformed Church the figure was 64 per cent.[9] These high figures also require explanation. One reason is the longer, more liberal tradition of thought about marriage in the mainstream Protestant denominations just described. Another reason is the contradictory messages that the Church of England has given out to divorced people in recent times. Some divorced people seeking a Christian wedding go to these churches partly because they are more confident that their requests will be honoured (even though sometimes they are not). Both these churches hold that marriage is a life-long commitment, but they also recognize that marriages can end. For different reasons a husband and wife can become estranged, and reconciliation between them can be impossible to achieve. In these circumstances the recognition that a failed marriage is over is not to 'put asunder' the parties to the marriage but to recognize that in fact the putting asunder has occurred already. Ministers in these churches are not obliged to enquire into what went wrong in the previous marriage, but to explore with them whether a further church wedding would be appropriate. The decision about this might take place in a short course of preparation for remarriage. Similar arrangements exist within the Church of Scotland.

So we can see that 'Those whom God has joined together, let no one put asunder' need not mean that marriage is indissoluble, or that the church has no authority to recognize divorce. God can recognize that a marriage can end, and so can churches. But what about that other scripture in Romans? Doesn't it state explicitly that a spouse may not remarry while the former partner is alive?

Not at all. St Paul was developing a powerful argument about how Christians who were formerly Jews should regard their former faith. He makes an obvious point that any law can only be binding on people when they are alive. He wants to say this in order to convince the Roman Christians that, in his words, they had 'died to the law' because in the new faith the law in the Hebrew scriptures no longer had authority over them. In the course of arguing this, he uses an example to illustrate that when you are dead you can't be bound by the law or by anything else. The example is the marriage law operating in the Jewish faith at the time. St Paul is not trying to establish a law. He is saying that Christians are free from the law because they have a new freedom in Christ. It is through Christ's death, not theirs, that they are free from the law. So the passage isn't about marriage or remarriage at all. One detailed study of the passage concludes: 'This illustration is not meant to teach us about divorce or remarriage.'[10] Exactly. So let's not worry in case it does.

The position of the Church of England on remarriage has until very recently been more complicated. This church is situated historically between the Roman Catholic Church and the more radical Protestant churches, and this is reflected in its attitude towards marriage. It retains from its Roman Catholic heritage more than an echo of the belief that marriage is indissoluble, yet it shares with Protestant churches both the recognition that marriages can end, with Protestant churches both that marriages can end, and that marriage in a strict formal sense should not be regarded as a sacrament. An influential working party explains the dilemma honestly. On the one hand, it says, 'Our own approach starts from the conviction ... that marriage is intended by God to be a permanent and life-long union, and must always be undertaken as such.' On the other hand, it says, 'But we do not hold the view that when a marriage has completely failed, it continues to subsist in a shadowy fashion: we believe that it can be said in a literal sense of two living people that they *were* married and are *no longer* married.'[11] In the last chapter we discovered a kind of thinking that tried to hold opposite poles in tension. Here is another example. Marriage is a permanent union. But some marriages, because they fail, are not permanent.

In brief, this is the developing position in the Church of England. Prior to November 2002, the official position was governed by a (1957) resolution, which stated:

> ... in order to maintain the principle of lifelong obligation which is inherent in every legally contracted marriage and is expressed in the plainest terms in the Marriage Service, the Church should not allow the use of that Service in the case of anyone who has a former partner still living.[12]

But as the report *marriage in church after divorce* explains, while this remained the formal position of the Church of England, it had moral but not legal force upon the clergy! Clergy who take the 'indissolubilist' position were not required to go against their consciences in marrying a divorced person. This position has not changed. However, in 1984 the bishops agreed:

1 that there are a substantial number in the Church who believe in good conscience that a 'second' marriage is possible in some cases;
2 that those clergy who take this considered view are free under the provision of civil law to allow such 'second' marriages and that a number are already doing so; and that
3 the ultimate decision in such cases must be a matter for the clergyman concerned. However the House hopes that clergy who wish to allow a 'second' marriage would seek the advice of their Bishops. The overall desire is to achieve as much pastoral consistency and fairness as possible in the current circumstances.[13]

In practice little pastoral consistency and fairness *was* achieved, for bishops and clergy differed both in conviction and practice about the matter, and there was little consistency between one parish and another, and one diocese and another.[14] By the 1970s some clergy were conducting what they called 'services of blessing', and in the 1980s, a 'service of prayer and dedication following a civil marriage' was introduced. This of course was not a marriage but a liturgical supplement to a civil marriage conducted elsewhere. So divorced people seeking remarriage in church may have found that they were offered either a full service, or the service of prayer and dedication, or neither. However, even in the Church of England (and the Church in Wales) 7,270 weddings involving a divorced person were solemnized in 1996, 10 per cent of all Anglican marriages in these two churches.[15]

In July 2002 the Church of England's 'parliament', the General Synod, passed a resolution affirming 'that there are exceptional circumstances in which a divorced person may be married in church during the lifetime of a former spouse'. The word 'exceptional' was added as an amendment in the debate, and great significance added to it. In November 2002 the General Synod at last took the step of repealing the old regulations and resolutions which stated that marriage was 'indissoluble save by death' and that the marriage service should not be used in the case of a divorced person whose former spouse was still alive. The Church of England's main newspaper, the *Church Times*, ran the story 'Divorce vote leaves choice to clergy', and announced: 'The General Synod has decided to leave it to the individual consciences of the clergy, informed by the Church's formularies and advice from the Bishops, whether or not in any particular case to officiate at church weddings for divorcees.'[16] For those dioceses which already have systems in place for allowing, in exceptional circumstances, further marriages, there will be little change. However if clergy did not consider offering further marriage services because of confusing regulations, they will now have to decide what their practice in future will be.

At the time of writing an explanatory statement about the present teaching of the Church of England is being prepared. It will be available as a leaflet from clergy and online from www.cofe.anglican.org. The leaflet will say

> The Church of England teaches that marriage is for life. It also recognises that some marriages sadly do fail and, if this should happen, it seeks to be available for all involved. The Church accepts that, in exceptional circumstances, a divorced person may marry again in church during the lifetime of a former spouse.

The leaflet advises you to talk to your local parish priest who will tell you whether he or she is prepared to consider the possibility of your further marriage. We will look at the questions you may be asked in the next section. If s/he is willing, in principle, to take things further, you and your intended spouse will be asked to complete an application form. You will then be invited to a confidential interview. The position of the Church of England then, has changed considerably, and very recently.

Should I marry in church a second time?

Let's move on from 'can I?' to 'should I?' marry in church a second time. As we have seen, if you are a widow or widower, the troublesome and complex issues that have been aired in this chapter *vis-à-vis* divorcees do not arise. If you love another person unconditionally, then marry him or her. The vows will leave no one in doubt about the nature of your new relationship. They will create space and assurance, which will help both of you to grow separately and together. You will want to seek the blessing of God upon your relationship, and you may already interpret your companionship with one another as a sure sign of God's love for both of you. Previous generations of Christians have been far less keen to commend a second marriage, but this reluctance was due mainly to the sway that the old ideas of marriage had upon the Christian mind. You were not supposed to be sexually active in later life, and after the fertile period, the justification of having children no longer applied. The likelihood of longevity, together with a greater understanding of sexuality, male and female, through the ageing process, help to dismiss these considerations. In any case, a further justification or positive outcome of marriage, from earliest times, was that of 'companionship', 'mutual comfort', or 'friendship'. A second marriage may offer these things in abundance. The priest who conducts your ceremony will want to be assured that you are ready for the big changes you are already planning, but this will be an expression of concern for you rather than a concern that your marriage conforms to church teaching.

If you remarry after divorce in a Protestant church, the position remains, of course, unchanged. Will 'further marriages' (as they are now called) in the Church of England now be more likely? Will people who are considering further marriage in the Church of England be more confident in seeking it? I hope so. How will it work? If the priest is not bound in conscience against the conduct of any further marriage and has invited you to fill in an application form, you are likely to discuss with him the questions which are contained in the explanatory leaflet. These are:

- What does marriage mean to you?
- What have you learned from your previous marriage?
- Has there been healing of past hurts?
- If you have children, how are they being looked after?
- What do others think of your marriage plans?
- When did your new relationship begin?
- Have either of you been divorced more than once?
- Are you wanting to grow in the Christian faith?

Clergy have received guidance from the bishops about how to handle these questions. For example, with regard to the first question they will want to know whether you understand that divorce is a breach of God's will for marriage. They will expect some indication that you or your partner will have grown in understanding as a result of the previous break-up, perhaps about yourself, or about what marriage is, about Christian values, about mistakes, and so on. Out of concern for the enduring of the new marriage they may seek some assurance that enough time has elapsed since the break-up for you to recover the emotional stability and sense of good judgement that may have been recently impaired.

At least one of the questions has a fairly obvious subtext. Were you having sex with your new partner when you were still married to your former spouse? That, of course, is adultery. You are unlikely to be asked that question with the same bluntness (and you may not be asked it at all). But you should know that all the churches understand adultery to be wrong. They base this view in part on the seventh of the Ten Commandments (Exodus 20:14) and on the way Jesus expounded it (Matthew 5:27–30). Marriage is a covenant (chapter 2) and adultery imperils it. Some priests may need assurance that you are not asking them (to use a common but unfortunate phrase) to 'consecrate an old infidelity'.

I wonder how you respond to these questions. Do you think they are too searching? Enough to put you off altogether? Or do you perhaps welcome them as a serious and thorough attempt to get to grips with difficult personal questions? I wonder also how the clergy will themselves apply them. The clergy will have little time (and probably little inclination) to pursue them very far. It has to be likely that the number of further marriages in the Church of England will increase steadily, in line with other Protestant churches. But these churches have largely abandoned the role of judge over whether a particular couple are worthy to receive a further, Christian marriage. It can be expected that a similar trend will happen in the Church of England. I think there may be other problems. For example, how does a priest know whether a couple has come to terms with the breakdown of the previous marriage? How does the couple know? How far can an analysis of the 'causes' of a marital breakdown be pressed? Even in the physical sciences it is very difficult to claim with much authority that a is the cause of b. With regard to human behaviour, especially if it has a long history, the identification of causal factors is fraught with difficulty. I hope that the prospect of discussing these questions will not prove too daunting. In its attempt to commend the permanence of marriage, the Church of England has sometimes appeared inflexible and uncaring to individuals who have requested further marriage or who have been marginalized or stigmatized even, by its teaching or its clergy. An impediment to change has now been removed.

The church, as we saw at the beginning, is concerned to commend the belief that marriage is in intention life-long, and so is rightly cautious about acting in such a way that divorce is reckoned to be 'normative'. So one way of reading these questions is as an assessment of one's own readiness for the big step. Just as the British tax system requires earners to self-assess their tax liability, further marriage may be an appropriate time for private self-assessment, both individually and with one's new partner. I can't help but think that the desire to seek the blessing of God upon a further marriage (provided it is in intention life-long) is itself given by God. Perhaps a growing number of the clergy also think this way.

A final point about the changes in the Anglican Church is that the 'service of prayer and dedication following a civil marriage', remains an option. It has not been withdrawn, and the use of it may be proposed if the priest is in the end unwilling to offer further marriage. You too may prefer it. But there is a definite sense of second-best about this, and some people have found a double standard in the church's unwillingness to solemnize a marriage on the one hand, and its willingness to surround a new marriage with an act of public worship on the other. Is it better than nothing, or worse than anything, because it is not the real thing? In the rest of the chapter let's contribute a few more thoughts to this private self-assessment.

First, if your former marriage failed, the idea of vocation (Chapter 3) may assume greater importance than it did the first time around. You will have your own 'take' on what went wrong, and this may help you to rethink whether you are 'called to', or suited for marriage. Can you, with God's help, keep your vows? If you were unable to live harmoniously with your former partner, can you live harmoniously with your new one? Perhaps you are more suited to living alone? What have you learned from your former marriage that you might carry over into a second marriage? Since marriage is an unconditional commitment, you may not be ready to make this, or you may even believe that it may never be right for you. I think it is fine (and potentially very honest) to come to this conclusion. It would mean that you are not called to marriage, so don't drift into it.

Second, it is important to stress that, according to the teaching of the Anglican, Protestant and Orthodox churches, it is possible to experience genuine release from former marital commitments that were sincerely made. The recent step taken by the Church of England provides confirmation of such release. This release is important in putting real psychological distance between you and your previous marriage. No, the bond that was your former marriage was not an indissoluble one, and you may think your recent experience of breakdown is painful proof enough of that. But there is a still stronger yet very simple reason that may reinforce the belief that the former marriage really is over. It derives from an insight[17] that a commitment no longer binds us to it when it has become impossible to keep. Suppose you promise someone a lift to the station, and your car refuses to start. Aren't you released from your promise? Sure there is a big gap between broken starter motors and broken marriages, but the logical principle is a similar one. You cannot be bound to a promise that you cannot keep. And some marriages really do degenerate into relationships where the promises made become impossible to keep. However much you may want to continue to love and cherish a marriage partner, that desire may become 'non-operational' if he (or she) is continually violent, or uncommunicative, or unfaithful to you. You cannot be bound by what you cannot help. If an intention becomes impossible to carry out, you are released from its obligations. You should resist the temptation to feel guilty about what you cannot prevent.

Third, there is a growing sense in the churches that their contribution towards helping people who are considering marrying again is to avoid all impression of negative judgement or grudging compliance, and instead to emphasize core Gospel values. These values include God's forgiveness of human wrongdoing, God's grace to empower human endeavour and God's power to renew human life after 'repentance', a genuine 'sorry-ness' for the mess we can make of our lives. Many people (rightly in my view) are turned right off when preachers bang on too much about our sinfulness, but there is an element of Christian talk about sin that resonates well with people who otherwise dislike it. That is the sense that even the most virtuous of people go wrong sometimes, and we have all experienced a gap between intention and action, between what we believe and what we do, between our hopes and the way things turn out. Paradoxically, the points where things have gone wrong in our lives can be the points where the seeking of God's help can be most effective. The Church is essentially a community of sinners (sainthood is very rare); so if there is stuff in your life that needs to be left behind, join the club! Let divine grace work!

Fourth (a similar point), the ending of a marriage can overwhelm people with all kinds of negative senses – of failure, remorse, rejection and worthlessness or 'dis-esteem'. It shouldn't be forgotten either that it can bring enormous relief. Either way it still takes courage to move on. If we are raising ourselves, however vulnerably, out of despair and into a new relationship of hope, the solemnization of the relationship as marriage, provided it is intended as a loving, life-long commitment, underwrites the intention. The blessing of God upon it 'seals' it.

Finally, we have seen that marriage exists not merely for our own and our children's sakes, it is a 'commonwealth' that contributes to the 'common good'. We have seen reason to be cautious about informal relationships, and about intimate relationships with less than full commitment. There is a social dimension to all our personal decisions, and opting for faithful, life-long marriage is to make a huge contribution to the common good.

We may have moved some way from the atmosphere of celebration and hope that permeated earlier chapters. We have had to think of failure, uncertainty and judgement. But the point of doing this was to indicate that springs of faith, hope and love can irrigate further marriages planted in God's forgiveness and love.

Notes

1. For a full discussion of the New Testament passages on divorce see Thatcher, *Marriage after Modernity*, Chapter 8. Readers wanting to take on a detailed analysis of these should try Instone-Brewer, D. (2002), *Divorce and Remarriage in the Bible: the Social and Literary Context*. Grand Rapids, MI, and Cambridge: Eerdmans.
2. For a convincing argument that indissolubility is not supported by ecclesiastical law, see Humphreys, J. and Taylor, S. J. (2002), 'Mystical union: legal and theological perspectives on marriage', in Thatcher (ed.), *Celebrating Christian Marriage*, pp. 421–39.
3. For a full description see Robbins, P. (2002), 'Marriage nullity in the Catholic Church: not every wedding produces a marriage', in Thatcher (ed.), *Celebrating Christian Marriage*, pp. 311–24.

4. Robbins, 'Marriage nullity in the Catholic Church', p. 318.
5. Accessed 12 December 2002. The website gives details of a helpline and a network of regional counselling centres.
6. For a full description of the Orthodox view of marriage and divorce, see Zion, W. B. (1992), *Eros and Transformation: Sexuality and Marriage: An Eastern Orthodox Perspective*. Lanham, MD: University Press of America.
7. These are, for 'unchastity' (Matthew 5:32 and 19:9), and when a believer is married to an unbeliever, and the unbeliever wants a divorce (1 Corinthians 7:12–16).
8. *Marriage in church after divorce: a discussion from a Working Party commissioned by the House of Bishops of the Church of England*. London: Church House Publishing (2000), p. 31. For a full explanation of the thinking, and the context, of this document by its chair, see Scott-Joynt, M. (2002),'Marriage, marriage after divorce and the Church of England: seeking coherent teaching and consistent practice', in Thatcher (ed.), *Celebrating Christian Marriage*, pp. 379–91.
9. *Marriage in church*, p. 33.
10. Instone-Brewer, *Divorce and Remarriage,* p. 210.
11. *Marriage in church,* pp. 11–12.
12. For the details of the Act of Convocation, see *marriage in church*, p. 27.
13. *Marriage in church*, p. 7.
14. For the sense of deep injustice that was often caused by this position see Woods, T. J. (2002), 'Contract or communion? A dilemma for the Church of England', in Thatcher (ed.), *Celebrating Christian Marriage*, pp. 392–402.
15. *Marriage in church*, p. 22.
16. On this, and on a record of the changes authorized by the General Synod in November 2002, see *Church Times*, 22 November 2002, pp. 15–16.
17. *Marriage in church*, pp. 46–7
18. Ibid, pp. 53–4
19. Convincingly argued by Margaret Farley (2002) in 'Marriage, Divorce and Personal Commitments', in Thatcher (ed.), *Celebrating Christian Marriage*, pp. 355–72.

Bibliography

Anderson, H. and Fite, R. C. (1993), *Becoming Married*. Louisville, KY: Westminster/John Knox Press.

Anglican Faculty Office. On-line at www.facultyoffice.org.uk.

Aquinas, T., *Summa Theologiae*.

Augustine, *On the Good of Marriage*, in Schoff, *The Nicene and Post-Nicene Fathers*, pp. 399–413.

Axinn, W. G. and Thornton, A. (2000), 'The transformation in the meaning of marriage', in Waite et al. (eds), *The Ties that Bind*, pp. 147–65.

Bailey, D. S. (1952), *The Mystery of Love and Marriage*. London: Camelot Press.

Bernard, J. (1972), *The Future of Marriage*. New York: Bantam Books.

Book of Common Prayer (1662), at www.eskimo.com/~ lhow ell/bcp1662/.

Brooke, C. (1989), *The Medieval Idea of Marriage*. Oxford: Clarendon Press.

Brown, P. (1989), *The Body and Society: Men, Women and Sexual Renunciation in Early Christianity*. London: Faber & Faber.

Brown, S. L. and Booth, A. (1996), 'Cohabitation versus marriage: a comparison of relationship quality', *Journal of Marriage and the Family*, 58 (August): 668–78.

Browning, D. S., Miller-McLemore, B. J., Couture, P. D., Lyon, K. B. and Franklin, R. M. (1997), *From Culture Wars to Common Ground: Religion and the American Family Debate*. Louisville, KY: Westminster John Knox Press.

Brundage, J. A. (1993), *Sex, Law and Marriage in the Middle Ages*. Aldershot: Variorum, Ashgate Publishing.

Burton, R. P. D. (1998), 'Global integrative meaning as a mediating factor in the relationship between social roles and psychological distress', *Journal of Health and Social Behavior*, 39: 201–15.

Catechism of the Catholic Church. London: Geoffrey Chapman (1994).

Catholic Information Network. Online at www.cin.org.

Celebration Hymnal for Everyone, Vol. 2. Great Wakering, Essex: McCrimmon, (1994).

Center for Marriage and Family website: www.creighton.edu/MarriageandFamily/.

Center for Marriage and Family, Creighton University, Omaha (2000), *Time, Sex, and Money: The First Five Years of Marriage*.

Center for Marriage and Family, Creighton University, Omaha (1995), *Marriage Preparation in the Catholic Church*.

Christian Copyright Licensing International. Online at www.ccli.co.uk.

Christian PREP® One-Day Workshop Leader Manual. Denver, CO (2000).

Christian Prevention and Relationship Enhancement Program (C-PREP) website: www.prepinc.com

Church of England website: www.cofe.anglican.org

Common Worship communion service. Online at www.cofe.anglican.org/commonworship/hc/intercessions. html. Accessed 14 November 2002.

Common Worship marriage service (Online version): www.cofe.anglican.org

Daly, M. and Wilson, M. (1994), 'Some differential attributes of lethal assaults on small children by stepfathers as opposed to genetic fathers', *Ethnology and Sociobiology*, 15: 1–11.

Davies, J. (1998), 'Neither seen nor heard nor wanted: the child as problematic. Towards an actuarial theology of generation', in Hayes et al., pp. 325–49.

—— (2002), 'Welcome the Pied Piper', in Thatcher, *Celebrating Christian Marriage*, pp. 240–49.

Dominian, J. (2001), *Let's Make Love: The Meaning of Sexual Intercourse*. London: Darton, Longman & Todd.

Facilitating Open Couple Communication, Understanding and Study [FOCCUS] website: www.foccusinc.com.

Farley, M. (2002), 'Marriage, Divorce and Personal Commitments', in Thatcher, *Celebrating Christian Marriage*, pp. 355–72.

Fotiou, S. (2002), 'Water into wine, and *eros* into *agape*: marriage in the Orthodox Church', in Thatcher, *Celebrating Christian Marriage*, pp. 89–104.

Gill, R. (1999), *Churchgoing and Christian Ethics*. Cambridge: Cambridge University Press.

Gillis, J. (1985), *For Better, for Worse: British Marriages, 1600 to the Present*. New York and Oxford: Oxford University Press.

Glenn N. (1997), *Closed Hearts, Closed Minds: The Textbook Story of Marriage*. New York: Institute for American Values.

Goldscheider, F. K. and Kaufman, G. (1996), 'Fertility and commitment: bringing men back in', *Population and Development Review*, 22 (suppl.): 87–99.

Goldscheider, F. K. and Waite, L. J. (1991), *New Families, No Families? The Transformation of the American Home*. Berkeley, CA: University of California Press.

Gray, J. (1993), *Men are from Mars, Women are from Venus: A Practical Guide for Improving Communications and Getting What you Want in your Relationships*. London: Thorsons.

Greeley, A. (ed.) (1979), *The Family in Crisis or in Transition: A Sociological and Theological Perspective*. Concilium, 121: New York: Seabury.

Guindon, A. (1986), *The Sexual Creators: An Ethical Proposal for Concerned Christians*. Lanham, MD: University Press of America.

Hatfield, E. (1988), 'Passionate and companionate love', in Sternberg and Barnes (eds), *The Psychology of Love*.

Hayes, M. A., Porter, W. and Tombs, D. (eds) (1998), *Religion and Sexuality*. Sheffield: Sheffield Academic Press.

Hogan, M. M. (1993), *Finality and Marriage*. Marquette Studies in Philosophy: Marquette, MI: Marquette University Press.

House of Bishops of the General Synod of the Church of England (1991), *Issues in Human Sexuality*. London: Church House Publishing.

Humphreys, J. and Taylor, S. J. (2002), 'Mystical union: legal and theological perspectives on marriage', in Thatcher (ed.), *Celebrating Christian Marriage*, pp. 421–39.

Instone-Brewer, D. (2002), *Divorce and Remarriage in the Bible: The Social and Literary Context*. Grand Rapids, MI, and Cambridge: Eerdmans.

Interchurch Families website: www.aifw.org.

Interfaith Marriages website: www.religioustolerance.org.

Isherwood, L. (2002), 'Marriage: haven or hell? Twin souls and broken bones', in Thatcher (ed.), *Celebrating Christian Marriage*, pp. 201–17.

John Paul II (1981), *Familiaris Consortio*. Vatican City: Vatican Press.

Juster, T. F. and Suzman, R. (1995), 'An overview of the health and retirement survey', *Journal of Human Resources*, 30.

Kippley, J. F. and Kippley, S. K. (1997), *The Art of Natural Family Planning* (4th edn). Cincinnati, OH: Couple-to-Couple League International.

Lake, S. (2000), *Using Common Worship: Marriage: A Practical Guide to the New Services*. London: Church House Publishing.

Lewis, J. (1999), *Marriage, Cohabitation and the Law: Individualism and Obligation*. London: Lord Chancellor's Department Research Secretariat.

Lewis, J. and Kiernan, K. (1996), 'The boundaries between marriage, nonmarriage, and parenthood: changes in behavior and policy in postwar Britain', *Journal of Family History*, 21 (July): 372–88.

Lord Chancellor's Advisory Group on Marriage and Relationship Support (2002), *Moving Forward Together, A Proposed Strategy for Marriage and Relationship Support for 2002 and beyond*. London: COI Communications. Also available at www.lcd.gov.uk.

Lord Chancellor's Department (1999), *The Funding of Marriage Support: a Review by Sir Graham Hart* (The Hart Report). Also available on www.lcd.gov.uk/family/fundingmarsup/reportfr.htm.

Macfarlane, A. (1987), *Marriage and Love in England: Modes of Reproduction 1300–1840*. Oxford: Basil Blackwell.

Mackin, T., SJ (1982), *What is Marriage?* New York: Paulist Press.

Marriage Care (in England and Wales): website: www.marriagecare.org.uk.

Marriage Resource website: www.marriageresource.org.uk.

marriage: a teaching document from the House of Bishops of the Church of England. London: Church House Publishing, (1999).

Methodist Worship Book. Peterborough: Methodist Publishing House (1999).

National Statistics Online. Online at www.statistics.gov.uk/.

'Notes on Marriage in the Church of England'. Available at www.cofe.anglican.org/lifechanges/index.html.

Oliver, M. A. M. (1994), *Conjugal Spirituality: The Primacy of Mutual Love in Christian Tradition*. Kansas City, KS: Sheed & Ward.

Outhwaite, R. B. (1995), *Clandestine Marriage in England, 1500–1800*. London and Rio Grande: Hambledon Press.

Parker, S. (1990), *Informal Marriage, Cohabitation and the Law, 1750–1989*. New York: St Martin's Press.

Peachey, P. (2001), *Leaving and Clinging: the Human Significance of the Conjugal Union*. Lanham, MD: University Press of America.

Popenoe, D. and Whitehead, B. D. (1999), *Should We Live Together? What Young Adults Need to Know about Cohabitation before Marriage: A Comprehensive Review of Recent Research*. The National Marriage Project, NJ: Rutgers, State University of New Jersey.

PREPARE/ENRICH website: www.lifeinnovation.com.

Prevention and Relationship Enhancement Program (PREP) website: www.prepinc.com.

RELATE website: www.byu.edu.

Rémy, J. (1979), 'The family: contemporary models and historical perspective', in Greeley (ed.), *The Family in Crisis*.

Revised English Bible. Oxford and Cambridge: Oxford University Press, Cambridge University Press (1989).

Robbins, P. (2002), 'Marriage nullity in the Catholic Church: not every wedding produces a marriage', in Thatcher (ed.), *Celebrating Christian Marriage*, pp. 311–24.

Ryle, G. (1963), *The Concept of Mind*. Harmondsworth: Peregrine Books.

Schoen, R. and Weinick, R. M. (1993), 'Partner choice in marriages and cohabitations', *Journal of Marriage and the Family*, 55 (May): 409.

Schoff, P. (ed.) (1887), *The Nicene and Post-Nicene Fathers*. Buffalo, IL: Christian Literature Co.

Scott, K. and Warren, M. (eds) (1993), *Perspectives on Marriage: A Reader*. New York: Oxford University Press.

Scottish Marriage Care website: www.scottishmarriagecare.org.uk.

Scott-Joynt, M. (2002), 'Marriage, marriage after divorce and the Church of England: seeking coherent teaching and consistent practice', in Thatcher (ed.), *Celebrating Christian Marriage*, pp. 379–91.

Social Research Unit, University of Surrey Roehampton for the Church of England Diocese of Guildford (March 2002), *Marriage and Adult Relationship Support in Southern England*.

Stanley, S. M. and Markman, H. J. (1992), 'Assessing commitment in personal relationships', *Journal of Marriage and the Family*, 54: 595–608.

Sternberg, R. J. (1988), 'Triangulating love', in R. J. Sternberg and M. L. Barnes (eds), *The Psychology of Love*. New Haven, CT: Yale University Press.

Stone, L. (1979), *The Family, Sex and Marriage in England 1500–1800*. London: Weidenfeld & Nicolson.

—— (1993), 'Passionate attachments in the West in historical perspective', in Scott and Warren, *Perspectives in Marriage*, pp. 171–9.

Stuart, E. (1995), *Just Good Friends: Towards a Lesbian and Gay Theology of Relationships*. London: Mowbrays.

Thatcher, A. (1998), 'Beginning marriage: two traditions', in Hayes et al. (eds), *Religion and Sexuality*.

—— (1999), *Marriage after Modernity: Christian Marriage in Postmodern Times*. Sheffield: Sheffield Academic Press.

—— (2002), *Living Together and Christian Ethics*. Cambridge: Cambridge University Press.

—— (ed.) (2002), *Celebrating Christian Marriage*. Edinburgh and New York: T. & T. Clark.

Time for Each Other (home video, available from *Marriage Resource*).

2-in-2-1. Marriage website: www.2-in-2-1.co.uk.

Tysoe, M. (1992), *Love Isn't Quite Enough: The Psychology of Male–Female Relationships*. London: HarperCollins/Fontana.

United States Law website: www.USLaw.com.

Waite, L. J., 'Trends in men's and women's well-being in marriage', in L. J. Waite, Bachrach, C., Hindin, M., Thomson, E. and Thornton A. (eds) (2000), *The Ties That Bind*. New York: de Gruyter, pp. 368–92.

Waite, L. J., Browning, D. S., Doherty, W. J., Gallagher, M., Luo, Y. and Stanley, S. M. (2002), *Does Divorce Make People Happy? Findings from a Study of Unhappy Marriages*. New York: Institute for American Values. Details are available online at www.amer icanvalues.org.

Waite, L. J. and Gallagher, M. (2000), *The Case for Marriage: Why Married People Are Happier, Healthier, and Better off Financially*. New York: Doubleday.

Wedding Guide UK website: www.weddingguideuk.com.

Wellings, K., Field, J., Johnson, A. M. and Wadsworth, J. (1994), *Sexual Behaviour in Britain: The National Survey of Sexual Attitudes and Lifestyles*. Harmondsworth: Penguin Books.

Whelan, R. (1993), *Broken Homes and Battered Children: A Study of the Relationship between Child Abuse and Family Type*. London: Family Educational Trust.

Witte, J., Jr (1997), *From Sacrament to Contract: Marriage, Religion, and Law in the Western Tradition*. Louisville, KY: Westminster John Knox Press.

Woods, T. J. (2002), 'Contract or communion? A dilemma for the Church of England', in Thatcher, *Celebrating Christian Marriage*, pp. 392–402.

Zion, W. B. (1992), *Eros and Transformation: Sexuality and Marriage: An Eastern Orthodox Perspective*. Lanham, MD: University Press of America.

Index

26, 28–30, 78, 99, 125, 127, 134

as a permanent lifelong commitment 10, 18, 20, 26, 38, 39, 49, 52, 54, 65, 70, 83, 84, 87, 99, 104, 133, 134, 136, 137, 138, 143, 144, 146

as a process 2, 69, 75, 77, 79, 81, 83–8, 99, 115

as a sacrament 37, 41, 119, 120, 123, 136, 138

as a vocation 46–7, 48, 66, 87, 144

as mutual devotion 36, 41, 52, 55, 104, 120, 128, 141

as the foundation of the family 26, 35

beginning of 76, 77, 81

breakdown of 16, 17, 20, 47, 87, 142, 143, 144

by ecclesiastical licence 93

civil 61, 91, 139

ethos of 128–130

impediments to 60, 92, 98

indissolubility of 80, 83, 135, 137, 139, 140

inter-church 59–60

inter-religious 60-1

of Christ to the church 30-1, 99

purposes of 32, 33, 34, 36, 56

registration of 81, 92, 98, 109

religious faith in 2, 61, 115, 118, 130

'spiritual death of' 136

vows 20, 25, 37, 40, 47, 49, 76, 79, 82, 87, 96, 98, 101, 103–5, 106, 108, 121, 123, 136, 141, 144

Marriage Care in England and Wales 63, 136

marriage enrichment 64

marriage preparation 2,45–66, 97, 118

Church of England 46, 79

Roman Catholic 45–6, 63, 75

Marriage Resource 63, 64

marriage service 2, 26, 76, 91, 94–112, 115

blessing 38, 84, 107–9, 141

Common Worship 25, 26, 31, 36, 37, 39, 40, 41, 56, 65, 94–112

declarations 98–9, 101

dismissal 112

giving and blessing of the rings 96, 105–7, 108

giving away the bride 101–3

hymns 2, 25, 96–7, 98, 109, 112

legal aspects 40, 46, 59, 61, 75, 76, 91–3, 98, 103, 109, 133, 139

meaning of 46, 59,

music 2, 97, 109, 112

order of service 39, 97

prayers 2, 25, 105, 106, 109, 110-12, 120, 121, 122, 124

proclamation of marriage 107

readings 2, 25, 31, 41, 75, 100-1

vows *see* marriage, vows

witnesses 40, 103, 109

masculinity, model(s) 58

mass, *see* holy communion

Methodist Church 137

marriage service 27, 30, 102

money 11, 16, 19, 48, 53, 57,